# REBOOT TO INTERFAITH

# REBOOT TO INTERFAITH

REV. DR. STEPHEN ALBERT

Waterside Productions

Printed in the United States of America

First Printing, 2020

ISBN-13: 978-1-949001-02-0 print edition
ISBN-13: 978-1-949001-03-7 ebook edition

Waterside Productions
2055 Oxford Ave
Cardiff, CA 92007
www.waterside.com

# DEDICATION

*This book is an extension of*
*the Interfaith experiences I have had since 2005.*
*And, it is really the extension of my life's direction*
*since 1947 which took me from*
*one good and/or bad experience to another.*
*Thank you God, for letting me serve you*
*in so many different capacities.*

*Thank you to all of my Interfaith friends*
*who have shared themselves with me*
*so that I could more easily understand how similar we all are.*

*Of all the people I have met over my lifetime,*
*no one has meant more to me than my wife Abigail.*
*I have observed from her actions*
*such incredible Compassion and Love*
*and the chance to explore and understand life*
*from a variety of simple and complex vantage points.*
*You have enriched my Soul*
*and I know our togetherness has touched the hearts of many.*
*Thank You*
*H&KE*

# TABLE OF CONTENTS

# AUTHOR'S NOTES:

*We do not want to convert any faith believer away from his or her faith's beliefs; rather we wish you to find the beauty in what you believe, and we respect you for honoring the best of your faith. At the same time, we want to make you aware of how, in the same way, others feel as passionate about their faith as you do about yours and that is all to the good. As someone said, "If you are going to be a Christian, be the best Christian you can be; If you are going to be a Jew, be the best Jew you can be; If you are going to be a Sikh, be the best Sikh you can be," and so forth. If you do not belong to a particular faith, be the best person you can be.*

⚜ ⚜ ⚜

While teaching an on-ground Comparative Religions class at the University of Phoenix one night, I encountered a reaction from one man about my discussion of Jesus being a Jew. "Jesus was <u>NEVER</u> a Jew!" he loudly expressed as he stood up and raised his Bible in defiance. When I countered his words with "everyone knows that Jesus was Jewish and that, in fact he was called Rabbi. "LIES!" he yelled, "Jesus was NEVER Jewish and he was NEVER a Rabbi!" His voice got louder and louder and I said, "Listen, do you believe what is in the Bible you have in your hand?" "This is the ABSOLUTE TRUTH!" he answered loudly. I calmly said, "Then open your Bible to John:6:25. and read what it says." He quickly opened his Bible and defiantly began to read: *(Disciples speaking to Jesus)* " … Rabbi, when did you come here?" The student sat down in silence.

**Moral: Love your faith AND study it so that you know the truth about it.**

10,000+
Faiths

# Preface

Have you ever felt WONDERFUL?

Hopefully, there has been at least one time in your life that you have felt absolutely GREAT! Your body felt strong; your head was clear; you knew exactly what you needed to do; and you felt that you had everything that you needed at that moment.

Can you remember those times? Peaceful, Huh?

REBOOT has become the term we use to get back to that time and begin to re-start our engine. On or off a computer, it gives us the peaceful opportunity to refresh our daily life. We can offset the times when we made a mistake or said the wrong thing at the wrong time. REBOOTING gives us a chance to forgive ourselves and/ or others for actions that seemed unfair or, in hindsight, wrong. Wouldn't you like to feel that way again? No matter how many mistakes you may have felt that you have made in your life, REBOOTing can open new avenues for you to experience happiness.

YOU ARE NOT ALONE! If you remember the story of Noah's Ark in the Bible, even God REBOOTED the world when *"God saw the wickedness of man was great in the earth…"* and, after the flood, *"I will remember my covenant which is between me and every living creature of all flesh."* So even God saw the beauty of *"all flesh"* and vowed never to have to REBOOT it again.

Whether you believe in Bible stories or not, every one of us has done something in our life which has caused us to have to REBOOT that portion of our life in some way. Sometimes that REBOOT is forced upon us. Whether it is going through a divorce or relationship change, having to change jobs, moving to another apartment, house, city, state or country, resolving financial issues or experiencing a major health challenge, we all experience REBOOTing.

On April 13, 2003, I suffered a severe stroke which left the entire left side of my body immobilized. From my face down to the bottom of my feet, all the muscles on the left side of my body stopped working. It took me 8 months of REBOOTING before I could drive again and almost a year before I felt almost normal.

Feeling "normal" or taking a breath from uncertainty to becoming peaceful, is probably the one goal every human faces at one time or another. Our personal balance becomes that much askew when we read the morning paper, listen to the TV news or have a conversation about the uneasy conditions in the world. When you do not know what to do next, when your world seems to be in chaos, having the faith to believe that it can get better can become your new normal. INTERFAITH is normal! Hating a person or group of people for not being like you is not! REBOOTING to INTERFAITH is the simplest thing we can do and it can return us to a life without stress and turmoil.

I was brought up in a slightly conservative Jewish family and I left the synagogue to study "religion" in more depth. My wife to-be, Abigail, grew up in a variety of Christian faiths. In the late 1980s, both of us, independently, found the New Thought Faith and chose to follow its teachings. At a Minister's conference in 1999, we met, fell in love, formed a church, got married and in 2005 discovered INTERFAITH. We helped form the Poway Interfaith Team in the city of Poway, California in 2006 and all our writings and speaking at conferences began to revolve around Interfaith.

One of the first summer programs the Poway Interfaith Team created was Interfaith Summer Nights. For 8 weeks, we scheduled a speaker from a different faith to come and educate us and the Poway community about their religion for 30-40 minutes. Then we would have community dialogue with questions and answers followed by refreshments. Every time we heard a different faith's speaker, Abigail would nudge me and say something to the effect of, "I believe that! I must be Buddhist!" This happened each week as we listened to the Hindu speaker, the Muslim speaker, the Jewish speaker and so on. Our awareness was heightened by not only hearing the speaker but also by meeting the members of their congregation who came with them. THEY WERE JUST LIKE US!

Our world today is less than peaceful. We hear about and sometimes meet people who think nothing about hating others to the point of shooting at them or running them down in the street while they are driving a car. Unfortunately, many times this is done using the guise of "religion" as a reason. Having thoroughly researched the various religions since 2005, I can tell you that NO RELIGIOUS AVATAR <u>EVER</u> PREACHED HATE – not Jesus, not Buddha, not Moses, not Muhammad; none of the Avatars taught his followers to hate.

This book is an introduction to the TRUTH about faith, religion and interfaith as a method to reduce your fears of interacting with people who might look or speak or act differently than you do. This is the chance for you to REBOOT and reduce your anxiety of living in an uncertain world.

Over
10,000
Distinct
Faiths

# FAITHS – Interfaith Harmony Teachings

**B**efore we list the various Faith's avatars and what their harmonious teachings were, we must recognize an important fact. The person who is worshipped today as the "symbol" of each faith, was **NOT** of that Faith! For example, Christianity began with the worship of Jesus, who was a Jew. The Lutheran Faith began with Martin Luther, who was a Roman Catholic. The Methodist Faith began with John Wesley, who was an Anglican. Bahá'u'lláh was not a Bahá'í', Buddha was not a Buddhist, Confucius was not a Confucian, Krishna was not a Hindu, Mahavira was not a Jain, Abraham was not a Jew, Lao-Tzu was not a Taoist, etc. The wonderful teachings of these avatars came BEFORE there was a religion honoring them. It was the followers of those masters who, after the death of the Avatar, created a religion and usually a dogma based on them. So, let's look at the harmonizing sayings of the masters BEFORE there was a religion about them.

## Bahá'u'lláh On Harmony

"People should act peacefully with high morals and benevolence with each other." "The entire human race is one." "Condemn and eradicate all forms of prejudice," *whether religious, racial, class or national including full equality for women– of opportunity, rights and privileges— with men;*

## Buddha On Harmony

"*Give up* wrong and harmful thoughts, words, and deeds by self-schooling etc.; *Replace them* by what would be healthy, good and useful to oneself and others in your thoughts, words, and deeds; *Uphold* good things, desires, and conditions and what is useful to good persons in general; and *Advance good and savory skills* and *prevent* what is unwholesome and bad, etc."

## Jesus On Harmony

"Blessed are the Peacemakers; they shall be called the children of God." "Judge not lest you be judged." (Matthew 7:1.) "Love your Neighbor as Yourself." (Matthew 22:39.)

## Muhammad On Harmony

"We should worship the only One God and treat all of God's creations with equality and compassion." "All humans are equal, regardless of race, gender, ethnicity or tribe."

## Mahavira On Harmony

"Be Tolerant – *All living beings, irrespective of their size, shape, and form, how spiritually developed or under-developed, are equal. We should love and respect them; show Kindness and Compassion to all.*"

## Abraham & Moses On Harmony

"You shall not murder." "You shall not commit adultery." "You shall not bear false witness against your neighbor." "You shall not covet your neighbor's house;"

## Native Americans On Harmony

"The One Great Spirit gave us the responsibility and guardianship of the earth." "Treat all things, living beings, animals, plants, inanimate objects, etc. with honor and respect."

## New Thought On Harmony

"Honor and respect all faiths, cultures, creeds, and races and learn from those who believe spiritual equity and human rights belong to everyone." "Foster a world that works for the highest good of all lives."

## Guru Nanak On Harmony

"EK Ong Kar" : We are all one, created by the One Creator of all Creation who is the Creator, Sustainer and Destroyer." "Reject all distinctions of caste, creed, race or sex and believe we are all equal."

## Lao-Tse On Harmony

"Do not Judge. *As soon as we judge one thing as beautiful, other things become less beautiful. Whether it is good or bad, it just is at that moment.*"

## Zarathustra On Harmony

"Live with each other with high morals, everyone being equal." "Each person should be free, no slavery." "Do not impose your religious views on other people with opposing views."

It is obvious that the Avatars, *from Whom the many different faiths were formed*, taught similar things about Creating Harmony with Others. If we choose to follow one faith or another, shouldn't we adhere to what the tenants of our faith are REALLY about?

# INTERFAITH – The Experience

Imagine attending a school reunion. There you meet people you knew years ago. You rationalize in your mind, "Do I look THAT old?" The truth is, they know you and you know them. You each remember some of the good and bad highlights of your time together. There are very few surprises. Now imagine yourself at a family reunion. All the aunts and uncles and cousins are there. Once again, you each remember some of the good and bad highlights of your time together. There are very few surprises.

Your experiences in both of these cases come from having some familiarization. You had experiences with these people. You celebrated and perhaps even mourned at times with these people. You have a degree of commonality with these people. Our perception of meeting people who are from a different faith and/or culture, can be one of unfamiliarity. We become uncomfortable because we do not know what to expect, how to act and how not to offend them. Are they friendly or must I protect myself? What if I say the wrong thing?

The truth is, they are just as scared of you! AND … they do not want to offend you either.

The most comfortable experiences we have had with new "non-us-type" people, is to sit down and share a meal together. We do not talk about religion first. We talk about our growing up, our schooling, our families, etc. We learn that we have much more in common than we had first thought. "You had two brothers? I had two brothers." You didn't like your 4th grade teacher? I didn't like my 4th grade teacher." "You want peace on Earth? I want peace on Earth." Before we mentioned religion, we were friends.

When you look at people who are not of your faith, religion or culture, you find out that they are HUMAN, just like you! They want their family to be safe and happy. They want their kids to go to good schools and perhaps college. They want to be healthy and to have all their friends and family experience a good and full life.

Thirteen months after my stroke in 2003, I began to volunteer at Palomar Hospital's Acute Rehab Center (ARC) in Escondido, California. In the many years I have been volunteering there, I have witnessed almost every type of stroke, brain injury, trauma and/or condition a person can rehab from. Men, Women, Black, White, Hispanic, Jewish, Christian, Muslim, 25 years old to 94 years young, it does not matter. Rich or poor, each patient goes through the same fears, confusion, and elations as they work their way through the rehab process to wellness. And each patient laughs with me as I greet them and ask how they are enjoying the hospital's gourmet food. "Yeah, the lobster tail is usually tough" I tell them. "And the filet mignon is always over done!" A smile goes a long way when a person, ANY PERSON, is experiencing a medical emergency.

Life is not particular; it does not play favorites. Obviously, a wealthy person may have a more lavish lifestyle than a person who has less wealth. But when it comes to normal life issues, we are more alike than different. We complain when the roof leaks, we struggle when our children want "stuff" we can't afford. And we laugh when younger people repeat the same concerns about life that we expressed when we were their age. If you grew up in a family which ate grits, grits will probably be one of the foods you will serve your children. If macaroni and cheese was part of your family's diet, you probably are serving it to your family today. If chutney was always on the menu, you are probably eating it tonight. Most of us become comfortable with the foods and conditions we experienced when we were young and continue having a similar lifestyle as we move forward.

For me, some of the best interfaith experiences I have had are when I am enjoying a traditional food dish from another faith or culture. Many times, I do not have any idea what I am eating but I am sure to be asking my host for the recipe before I leave. Do you remember when your family first went out to a different style of restaurant other than what you were used to at home? For me it was Chinese food. I remember as a pre-teen, my Jewish mother thoroughly enjoying the Won Ton soup she was sipping even after being told that it had pork in it. My Italian-Catholic next-door neighbors always had wonderful cooking smells coming out of their home. Then I learned that in almost every culture and religion, PASTA is one of the most common diet staples. Whether you wrap pasta with meat, fish, chicken, vegetables or just boil it and top it with ANY type of sauce you enjoy, anyone would feel comfortable at anyone else's kitchen table. Pasta is an Interfaith food.

We are all alike! As children, our growing-up experiences cause us to mistakenly believe that ALL people are having the exact same experiences as we; and they are not. The more different our experiences are as children, and the faith(s) that we are raised with, the more open we become to appreciating the life and lifestyle of others. The amount of travel we do, the many different places that we visit, the discrimination we face, the love and violence we see within our family and/or in our community – all of this makes us who we are. Good or bad, WITHOUT JUDGMENT, we finally have a way to REBOOT our life through INTERFAITH.

# POWER, NOT A RELIGION

Now again, please remember that INTERFAITH is not a religion. It is actually the POWER we need to REBOOT this world. It is an opportunity to recognize the beauty of the world's people and the loving consciousness that exists deep within each of our souls. Interfaith is natural and non-judgmental. It is loving and comfortable and non-aggressive. In a warm and peaceful, friendly manner, it is a family of joy-filled and supportive people who are kind and cooperative. They are fun and wanting to help each other experience all the good that life has to offer. All you need to do is to reach out and experience the love as you REBOOT your thinking to accept greater possibilities for yourself, your family and friends.

We need to re-examine our thinking about "Those People" and recognize that "those people" are also us. In 1986 I coined the word "PEOPLEism" which became the title of my first book. I defined it as follows:

# PEOPLEism PEOPLE-ISM
## (PE'P'LIZ'M)

1. The theory of the ownership and operation of the world by all people working together to create a productive, efficient, interesting, and secure society.
2. The belief in people of all disciplines of study helping each other with their expertise and experience.
3. People creating a better future by working together through understanding.

Again. INTERFAITH DOES NOT ASK YOU TO ABANDON THE FAITH YOU WERE BORN INTO.

In fact, interfaith asks you to LOVE the faith you live by and, at the same time, accept that others who come from other faiths feel as strongly about their faith as you do about yours.

I knew PEOPLEism was possible in 1986 and, I know it is possible today. Developing Personal Power is the motivating force of all people. Everyone, in his or her own way, strives to gain as much power as possible. An infant discovers power when his or her small cry brings an adult running in the middle of the night. A two-year-old finds the word "No!" said loudly enough, will get him what he wants or allow him to eliminate what he does not want at the dinner table. Then he is at peace. As we get older, no matter what our faith, culture, race, or income level, our attempts to gain power increases.

Remember crossing the street without your parents' permission or coming home in the evening later than curfew. In every instance we tried to gain more power. During those early years there are so many others telling us what we could and could not do, it is a wonder that more younger people do not become problem teens or even haters. Were you ever told, "OUR people do not do those things"? "Be careful driving through THAT neighborhood". "OUR church/God is the only right way to live." What we were told, correct or not, may have stifled our growth for years.

A high school college counselor told me when I was sixteen that I was not college material. She said I should apply at a trade school to further my education. Because I did not believe her, I earned three college degrees and a Doctor of Religious Studies. However, I wonder how many other high school students allowed her to take control of their ambitions and, today, have yet to reach their potential.

Being a teenager is difficult enough due to the physical and emotional changes which occur. Not being permitted to question your family's spiritual life or daily habits may have reduced your power and can be extremely frustrating. Were your teenage years peaceful? Remember how mature you felt at seventeen? Remember how you felt you knew everything about life? We learned by our mistakes and without having the chance to make those mistakes, we would not have grown to where we are today. How have you changed?

Some rules are made to control people and are important for the good of everyone. Directional traffic signs and speed controls are posted to protect the rights of most people in society. Rules governing minimum length of education and topics taught in school ensure a proper level of education for everyone. However, as each rule is made, every person senses a lose of power and control. It is no wonder people become power hungry.

In the quest for power, no matter of which faith or culture you come from, people can become selfish. It is this selfishness which is destroying their chances of obtaining ULTIMATE POWER. What is Ultimate Power? Ultimate power gives us everything we want and, at the same time, does not take anything away the sense of peace from anyone else. It is the power stemming from the belief in people and knowing their growth will only help ours. This is INTERFAITH! When we experience ultimate power, we become human again and are capable of obtaining unlimited security both within ourselves and within our environment. It is by resurrecting the deep-hidden peace we experienced as a child, that we find the truth to be peace-filled and happy.

# REBOOT "Those People" Thinking

If there is one area of life which causes a great deal of anxiety for the average human, it is facing "the unknown." The unknown, no matter of what type, creates a degree of fear which automatically sets up a mental, emotional and physical response in our body. Going for a job interview, meeting the in-laws for the first time, buying a new home, going for follow-up tests at the doctor's office, all can be very stressful no matter what your faith. ***WHAT'S UNDER THE BED?*** Very young children can be fearful of anything and, as such, what they learn to fear is whatever their family and peers fear or whatever causes them pain. **FEAR IS A LEARNED BEHAVIOR** and when your familial society emphasizes you should be fearful of something or some group of people, most people go along with the premise that their family and friends are doing the correct thing. Unfortunately, many of those fears are unwarranted.

When the unknown becomes known, then we have no fear.
Entering a dark house can be scary, until we switch on the light.
A problem can only be solved when we become aware of its source.

Like so many teenagers of the 50's and 60's, I learned that the unknown does not have to be fearful if you approached it as if you were NOT going to create pain for yourself. Why couldn't meeting new people be enjoyable? In college I went to my first Christmas party and learned the friendships which I made there went beyond religious beliefs. To EXPECT trouble and pain made no sense to me. Pain can happen in any good or bad situation and the prejudice we pre-ordain for ourselves comes from what we were taught as children by our family and friends. We impose this pain upon ourselves and our children in an effort to eliminate a "possible pain" which really does not exist. We can change that behavior and we must.

Some wonderful experiences you might like to participate in during the year include: Breaking the fast at Ramadan with Muslims, Lighting the candles with Jews at Chanukah, Lighting fireworks with Hindus at Diwali, Lighting candles with people of African descent during Kwanzaa, Decorating a Tree with Christians at Christmas, Experiencing a devotional with people from the Baha'i faith. And there are so many more experiences to choose from throughout the year. Are you willing to bring LIGHT into your life?

I learned that most of the world is even alike when we are in mourning. People's beliefs about what happens when we die may be different yet occur with people within any faith. Note: This is a great topic for discussion when you meet people of any faith. The fact is, if you filled a room with dozens of people from each faith, each wearing a white tee-shirt and blue jeans, you would never know who is from what faith. And if you entered the room knowing everyone was just as caring as you are, why would you be fearful? There would be no unknowns. The fear would be gone, and you would want more time to make friends with everyone. **We have to grow up and become friends.**

Young children do not have the fears adults have when they interact with new people. If children were placed in a room with dozens of children from other religions from around the world, they would be playing games with each other within minutes. When you are not anticipating anything unknown, you begin to enjoy the interaction. In this vein I ask you to: Act as a little child so you can enter the kingdom of peace with "Those People."

I have made it my goal to learn to eliminate my ignorance about other faiths, cultures, races and religions in an effort to eliminate the "unknown" about "THOSE PEOPLE." We are too much alike to focus only on the difference of the color of our skin or the language we speak. Yes, we dress differently, and we have different rituals which we use to celebrate our religion. That does not take away from all the similarities we have in common. It also does not take away from all the concerns we each have for our families and for the world. I stand back when I hear or read about the violence and hatred people around the world impose on others who they really do not know. I pray each one of them takes the steps necessary to learn the similarities of all the faiths rather than relying on the inaccurate facts they had been told as a child. This is where Interfaith comes in.

# THE GOLDEN RULE – AN INTERFAITH TOOL

D ID YOU KNOW…only 31% of this world is Christian and "The Golden Rule" appears in almost <u>every</u> religion's holy texts? These facts must be stated so that one faith does not feel they are the majority and, that almost all the faiths have something in common.

Almost every religious group has a version of the Golden Rule in their holy text. Yet when we see one of "THOSE PEOPLE" we only look at their few differences like skin color or language rather than the many similarities. When we spend time to listen to "THOSE PEOPLE," we learn they are almost exactly the same as we are. **Violence on this planet MUST STOP** and the only way we can do this is to eliminate "THOSE PEOPLE" thinking and focus on Interfaith.

According to the Christian Encyclopedia, there are over 10,000 distinct Religions in the world and over 33,800 Christian Branches. Truthfully, there are more problems with <u>INTRA</u>faith than INTERfaith. In Luke: 6:41, Jesus asks, "Why do you look at the speck of sawdust in your brother's eye and pay no attention to the plank in your own eye?" More people will accept others from a different faith before they will accept people of their own faith who worship differently. Yet they all say they agree with the Christianity's Golden Rule which says "Do unto others as you would have them do unto you." Here is a sample of Golden Rules as taught in 22 different faith groups. Read them and FEEL the similarities:

## Baha'i:

*"Ascribe not to any soul that which thou wouldst not have ascribed to thee, and say not that which thou doest not." "Blessed is he who preferreth his brother before himself."* Baha'u'llah

## Brahmanism:

*"This is the sum of Dharma [duty]: Do naught unto others which would cause you pain if done to you".* Mahabharata, 5:1517*"*

## Buddhism:

*"... a state that is not pleasing or delightful to me, how could I inflict that upon another?"* Samyutta NIkaya v. 353 .      *Hurt not others in ways that you yourself would find hurtful."* Udana-Varga 5:18

## Christianity:

*"Therefore all things whatsoever ye would that men should do to you, do ye even so to them: for this is the law and the prophets."* Matthew 7:12, King James Version. *"And as ye would that men should do to you, do ye also to them likewise."* Luke 6:31, King James Version. *"... and don't do what you hate..."*, Gospel of Thomas 6. The Gospel of Thomas is one of about 40 gospels that were widely accepted among early Christians, but which never made it into the Christian Scriptures (New Testament).

## Confucianism:

*"Do not do to others what you do not want them to do to you"* Analects 15:23 *"Tse-kung asked, 'Is there one word that can serve as a principle of conduct for life?' Confucius replied, 'It is the word 'shu' — reciprocity. Do not impose on others what you yourself do not desire.'"* Doctrine of the Mean 13.3 *"Try your best to treat others as you would wish to be treated yourself, and you will find that this is the shortest way to benevolence."* Mencius VII.A.4

## Ancient Egyptian:

*"Do for one who may do for you, that you may cause him thus to do."* The Tale of the Eloquent Peasant, 109 – 110 Translated by R.B.

Parkinson. The original dates to 1970 to 1640 BCE and may be the earliest version ever written.

## Hinduism:

*This is the sum of duty: do not do to others what would cause pain if done to you.* Mahabharata 5:1517

## Humanism:

*"(5) Humanists acknowledge human interdependence, the need for mutual respect and the kinship of all humanity." "(11) Humanists affirm that individual and social problems can only be resolved by means of human reason, intelligent effort, critical thinking joined with compassion and a spirit of empathy for all living beings." "Don't do things you wouldn't want to have done to you,"* British Humanist Society.

## Islam:

*"None of you [truly] believes until he wishes for his brother what he wishes for himself."* Number 13 of Imam *"Al-Nawawi's Forty Hadiths."*

## Jainism:

*Therefore, neither does he [a sage] cause violence to others nor does he make others do so."* Acarangasutra 5.101-2. *"In happiness and suffering, in joy and grief, we should regard all creatures as we regard our own self."* Lord Mahavira, 24th Tirthankara *"A man should wander about treating all creatures as he himself would be treated.* "Sutrakritanga 1.11.33

## Judaism:

*"... thou shalt love thy neighbor as thyself.",* Leviticus 19:18 *"What is hateful to you, do not to your fellow man. This is the law: all the rest is commentary."* Talmud, Shabbat 31a. *"And what you hate, do not do to any one."* Tobit 4:15

## Native American Spirituality:

*"Respect for all life is the foundation."* The Great Law of Peace. *"All things are our relatives; what we do to everything, we do to ourselves. All is*

*really One.*" Black Elk "*Do not wrong or hate your neighbor. For it is not he who you wrong, but yourself.*" Pima proverb.

## New Thought:

"*What we do unto others will be done also to us – The Law of Cause and Effect.*" (*The 10 Core Concepts of Science of Mind, Ernest Holmes, Pg.2*)

## Roman Pagan Religion:

"*The law imprinted on the hearts of all men is to love the members of society as themselves.*"

## Shinto:

"*The heart of the person before you is a mirror. See there your own form*" "*Be charitable to all beings, love is the representative of God.*" Ko-ji-ki Hachiman Kasuga

## Sikhism:

*Compassion-mercy and religion are the support of the entire world*". Japji Sahib "*Don't create enmity with anyone as God is within everyone.*" Guru Arjan Devji 259 "*No one is my enemy, none a stranger and everyone is my friend.*" Guru Arjan Dev : AG 1299

## Sufism:

"*The basis of Sufism is consideration of the hearts and feelings of others. If you haven't the will to gladden someone's heart, then at least beware lest you hurt someone's heart, for on our path, no sin exists but this.*" Dr. Javad Nurbakhsh, Master of the Nimatullahi Sufi Order.

## Taoism:

"*Regard your neighbor's gain as your own gain, and your neighbor's loss as your own loss.*" T'ai Shang Kan Ying P'ien. "*The sage has no interest of his own, but takes the interests of the people as his own. He is kind to the kind; he is also kind to the unkind: for Virtue is kind. He is faithful to the faithful; he is also faithful to the unfaithful: for Virtue is faithful.*" Tao Teh Ching, Chapter 49

## Unitarian:

*"We affirm and promote respect for the interdependent of all existence of which we are a part."*

## Wicca:

*"An it harm no one, do what thou wilt"* (i.e. do whatever you will, as long as it harms nobody, including yourself). One's will is to be carefully thoughtout in advance of action. This is called the Wiccan Rede

## Yoruba: (Nigeria):

*"One going to take a pointed stick to pinch a baby bird should first try it on himself to feel how it hurts."*

## Zoroastrianism:

"That nature alone is good which refrains from doing unto another whatsoever is not good for itself". Dadistan-i-dinik 94:5 "Whatever is disagreeable to yourself do not do unto others." Shayast-na-Shayast 13:29

# THE PROBLEM WITH
# THE GOLDEN RULE

"Treat people the way YOU want to be treated." Sounds great huh? However, many people may not want to be treated the way you do. For instance, in the New Thought faith it is quite common for anyone to hug a person they meet in or out of a religious setting. In Islam a man may only hug a woman from his own family. In fact, Islamic men are never even to shake hands with a woman of ANY faith outside their family. An orthodox male Rabbi, likewise, may only hug a female from his own family and may not shake hands with other females. A man outside the Hindu faith may not hug a female from that faith who is not of his family. To be safe, when you do not want to accidently insult someone you do not know, either place your palms together in front of your heart in a 'Namaste' position when you meet the person, or place your hand to your heart as you nod to them. In Interfaith, the Golden Rule has been replaced by the Platinum Rule which is: "Treat people the way THEY want to be treated." This will be covered in depth in the Supplemental Material section of this book.

## REBOOT Steps to Peaceful Relationships With Others

I once consulted for a Human Relations Vice President of a large corporation who told me in confidence, she loved her job except for one thing, she hated to deal with the employees! Did you know

65% of the managers in U.S. corporations hate their jobs? The reason ... they have to deal with people. The divorce rate in the U.S. is over 50%. The reason? People have NOT been taught from childhood about how to communicate with another person. We are not taught how to speak effectively, how to listen, how to take criticism nor how to give criticism in a manner which will not offend. And can you imagine the increase in miscommunication when there is a language or cultural barrier to deal with? Interfaith insults can happen by very caring people who do not know the rules of how not to insult someone of a different religion or faith.

# How Not to
## Offend – Generalities

Many people can agree on one thing or another but there is no area in which everyone agrees. As much as we want EVERYONE to realize how important our goals and missions are, their priorities may be different than ours. If you were stranded on an island and needed to know life-sustaining techniques, your political truths would probably not help you survive. If your doctor told you that you had less than a month to live, perhaps your desires to save a dying species of fungi elsewhere on this planet would not be the first thing on your mind. If you stood before your home after a hurricane, tornado or fire had consumed it, saving the rain forest or feeding the homeless might not be the vital issue for you at that moment. So it is with regard to Interfaith.

The truth is, there are billions of "causes" which a person can get attached to, and each one has its importance. Saving women, children and other humans from physical abuse, reducing poverty and crime in our neighborhoods, finding a cure for Cancer, A.I.D.S., Multiple Sclerosis, Parkinson's, Alzheimer's, and so on, are each important. So are working with the Boy and Girl Scouts, being a Big Brother or Big Sister to help kids in need, volunteering at a hospital or church or neighborhood out-reach organization or the many causes which have world-wide impact. All are wonderful causes for persons to spend their time working for. There are people who will tell you that the most important thing in the world for them is that their local sports team wins a game. Others who will tell you that nothing is more important than their favorite TV show staying on the air for another season. In every field, occupation, hobby and area of life, people choose to rally around a cause which speaks to them, and the fact that they want to help "whichever," is a noble deed. What reduces the nobleness is when one person believes that their cause is more important than your cause. Unfortunately, in our world today, this could include a person being willing to kill you because you have a different skin color, dress differently or speak with a different accent. Rather than spending the time to listen to what you believe and accepting that it is you, some people would prefer to do violence than to give you that privilege.

Years ago, I saw a portion of a mid-day television show where regular (?) people on a panel were talking about what was attractive to them in a romantic partner. One very obese man was attracted only to partners who were petite and shorter than five feet. One very short, small man was attracted only to partners taller than six feet. One woman would date only bald-headed men and one person would date only outside their own race. The discussion went on for too long and for me served only to drive home the point that each person has their own likes and dislikes, their own truths. *Aside from those whose truths exist to consciously damage others*, if someone's truths work for them, fine! I choose not to judge if someone else's truth is a "correct" truth. I would hope each person would do the same for me. Once a person does violence against another, the entire focus changes.

This book is about recognizing that all people have a right to be respected and honored for who they are and for the positive deeds that they do. Since we are all human, our first and primary task is to recognize that fact. In general, when you first meet new people from ANY faith, avoid talking about: Politics, Sex, Women's rights, Abortion, Gay rights, and other controversial subjects <u>unless they bring it up first</u>.

As you become more accepting of Interfaith and venture out to meet others from different faiths, I have listed some of the general traits of those faiths, especially with regard to worship. When you meet with individual congregants, they may or may not adhere to all of the facts mentioned. For example, I have a Rabbi friend who tells his Jewish congregation, "I know that some of you order pepperoni or sausage on your pizzas; please don't tell me about it!" I have been asked many times, "Why do men and women sit separately at so many faith services." The answer…A Worship service is a time for your mind to be focusing on WORSHIP. Socializing or looking around for a partner to date can happen after the faith service. Especially in an Islamic service, the male congregants at times sit in a prone position on their knees with their forehead on the floor in front of him. This places the worshipper's head only a foot behind the butt of the man kneeling in front of him. If this was the butt of a woman, his concentration on God could be distracted. Here are some of the Faith generalities:

In the **Baha'i faith,** they believe in modesty in all things. There is no discrimination of any sort. No gambling of any sort is permitted. During worship, there are no head covering required and no offering are taken from guests during the services. The Baha'is have no dietary restrictions.

In the **Buddhist faith**, many are vegetarians. No shoes are allowed in the Temple and there are no head coverings required during worship. There is no touching especially with people from the opposite sex. A slight bow with your hands palms-together in the Namaste position is always appropriate for all you meet. Please do not wear replicas of other religious symbols or figures while in the temple. No offering is taken from guests during the services.

In the **Christianity faith,** no head covering is required during worship. There are no dietary restrictions. Rituals will differ in various denominations. A collection plate will be passed around during the service to receive monetary offerings.

In the **Confucian faith,** many are vegetarians. Societal chaos & lack of civility is abhorred. No shoes are worn in the Temple and no head covering is required. No offering is taken from guests during the services.

In the **Hindu faith,** the cow is a holy animal and therefore there is no beef in the Hindu diet. Most Hindus are vegetarian. Shoes are not worn in their Temple and the orthodox do not shake hands with people of the opposite sex. No offering is taken from guests during the services.

In the **Islamic faith,** no fancy clothing is worn. Men and women cover their arms and legs in the Mosque and everyone wears a head covering. Abusing others is considered one of the worst traits a person can do. No shoes are worn in the Mosque and men and women sit separately. No offering is taken from guests during the services. There is no physical contact between men & women while in the mosque. Pork products and alcohol are prohibited in their Halal diet.

In the **Jain faith**, all follow a vegetarian diet and eat simple foods. They avoid emotional disturbances and live a non-violent lifestyle. Perfumes or scents are not used and they consider all living things as precious and avoid disturbing them. Prayers for forgiveness are on-going in case an insect or any life form had been accidentally hurt by their actions. This includes a bug being killed on the windshield of their car when driving.

In the **Jewish faith,** believing that the Holocaust never happened is an insult. Their Kosher diet includes no pork or shellfish. In the Temple, men (and in some Temples women also), wear a head covering and everyone stands when the Ark is opened. In orthodox Temples, men & women sit separately. Dress is wearing modest clothing and jewelry. No offering is taken from guests during the services.

In the **Native American faith,** it is expected that everyone will respect and obey all Indian laws. Different Tribes Have different food restrictions so ask before you visit. There is no photography allowed on the reservation. No alcohol or drugs are permitted on the reservation. When you are on Indian soil, you are on "Indian Time" and watches are not worn. Looking at your watch is an insult. Activities will take as long as they need to take during that time.

In the **New Thought faith,** there is no discrimination of any sort. No head covering is worn during worship. A collection plate will be passed around during the service to receive monetary offerings. There are no dietary restrictions and the dress is business casual. There is an emphasis to avoid drugs & over-indulgences. New Thought congregants are taught, and believe, that God resides in each person they meet.

In the **Sikh faith,** most are vegetarian. No shoes are worn in the Temple and all men & women sit separately and wear a head covering. No offering is taken from guests during the services. Modest clothing is expected of guests although dresses worn by Sikh woman come in bright colors.

In the **Tao faith,** most people are vegetarians. No shoes are worn in the Temple and people do not use or wear religious figures or jewelry in the Temple. No offering is taken from guests during the services.

# INTERFAITH PEACE 12-STEP PROGRAM

On June 10, 1935, William Griffith Wilson and Dr. Robert Holbrook Smith created an organization called Alcoholics Anonymous (AA). The purpose was to help alcoholics not to drink. Stemming from a spiritual experience by Wilson, it contained a Twelve Step spiritually based program of recovery for alcoholism. It has been the most successful recovery program in the world and has been duplicated by many other recovery organizations. With a membership of over two million people, AA is a wonderful example of how to assist people who wish to create a better life for themselves. With the over 100 other 12-Step organizations in the world, I estimate there are over eight million people in the world who attended some type of 12-Step meeting every week.

The 12-Steps is a process which works to heal people from alcoholism, gambling, codependency, overeating, negative emotions, being in debt, narcotics, overly sexual tendencies, and numerous other obsessions. It can change one's mind and life from perpetuating problems to resolving problems. **I believe it can be the methodology**, through INTERFAITH, to bring about Peace on Earth and peace in your life. Therefore, I have edited the 12-Steps and created a program which is dedicated towards World Peace. The word "God" is used in place of Spirit, Higher Power, Allah, God of my Understanding, etc. for simplicity. The words on the following pages may become the credo by which all the people of this world come into a peaceful balance.

**Step 1.** I surrender to God's direction in my life to help establish Peace on Earth for the good of all.

**Step 2.** I accept myself as a child of God and honor myself and others with peace, respect and love.

**Step 3.** I accept and receive each person I meet as a child of God and honor them with peace, respect and love.

**Step 4.** I forgive myself and others for past actions which hurt others.

**Step 5.** I forgive myself and others for past actions which, I felt, hurt me.

**Step 6.** I am entirely ready to have God remove any defects of character which reduce the possibilities of Peace around me.

**Step 7.** I humbly ask God to remove any blockages within me to creating Peace around me.

**Step 8.** I make a list of all people with whom I am not at peace and become willing to make amends to them all.

**Step 9.** I make direct amends to all people with whom I am not at peace.

**Step 10.** I continue to take personal inventory and, when I cause a situation not to be peaceful, I promptly admit it.

**Step 11.** I seek through prayer and meditation to improve my conscious contact with God as I understand God, praying only for knowledge of God's peaceful will for me and the power to carry it out.

**Step 12.** Having had a change in consciousness as a result of these steps, I choose to carry the message of Peace to others and to practice these principles in all my affairs.

## How to Work the 12-Steps

It is one thing to read the 12-Steps and say "yes, this makes sense to me." It is another thing to understand how to use the Steps in your life. The following is a Step-by-Step description of how to personalize your steps towards inner and outer Peace.

# Step One

*I surrender to God's direction in my life to help establish Peace on Earth for the good of all.*

This first step is one of the most difficult steps for some people because it contains the word "surrender." To many people, surrender means giving up POWER – to be powerless! Yet as we examine it more closely as it is used in this context, it is exactly the opposite.

Have you ever played peek-a-boo with a small child? When children place their hands over their eyes, they are gone. In their minds they are not there – you cannot see them. They have the power to transform themselves, in their mind, to someplace else. They surrender to their own inner power to transform themselves into the invisible. As adults, we see this as a game. It is fun and brings much laughter. For the child, it is real. Their inner God presence does not question what can or cannot be done. Everything is possible. So it is with Step One.

Our surrender to God's direction in our lives does not make us powerless. It is the process by which we change our consciousness and become open to the possibilities of being powerful enough to create the conditions we desire in our lives. It is giving up the appearance of lack and limitation and the absence of Peace and, instead, consciously believing the truth that Peace is happening now and this truth is created by a power beyond our explanation or full understanding. When we admit to ourselves and "know" the higher power WITHIN US can create the Peace we seek, we become powerful. The child's simple belief that they are invisible, makes it so. Are you willing to believe the God Presence within you / your spiritual guide is powerful enough to establish Peace between you and people of other faiths? If so, you are on your way to World Peace for the good of all. In all twelve of these steps it is important to realize YOU are in charge. YOU decide when to believe, when to let go, when to forgive when to accept your free-will to create the life and world you desire. Only YOU can do it! Each parent wants the best for their children and hopes they will not succumb to drugs or violence. No matter how much a parent always prays for their child to make the proper choices, it is up to the child to make those on-the-spot decisions. So it is with us.

God, Spirit, or whatever you call your higher consciousness, offers guidelines for children's growth. However, as his children, WE can choose to ignore those guidelines at any time. WE can follow a path of self-destruction or of humble acceptance. WE, by accepting these Steps into our conscious prayer time and our conscious awakened time, can move away from unhappiness and enjoy a life of joy and peace with the peoples of the world.

## Step Two

> *I accept myself as a child of God and honor myself with peace, respect and love.*

Step Two sets up a "present tense" mental process of acceptance of our self for our own good. In a world where people put themselves down for being too fat, too short, too old, too young, too dumb, too whatever – in a world which accepts war as "part of life", full acceptance of our self is rarely found. In fact many people will accept other people's frailties yet not their own.

As we realize we were created in the image and likeness of God, and accept the Spirit of God as being absolute good, we can only conclude God can ONLY create good in everything. As his children, we have no choice but to be part of that good and therefore need to learn to honor ourselves with peace, respect and love. We also need to do that with everyone else we meet.

How do you love yourself? It is difficult when we allow the media to convince us about what is beautiful and correct. Are you the right dress size? Do you have enough muscle tone? Does your tummy bulge a little more than it used to? Notice that the things the media emphasizes is APPEARANCE. The soul of us is not our appearance. Beautiful people exist in not so model-like bodies and, to love ourselves and others, we must look beyond the body and into the soul. The peace, respect and love we need to develop for our self and others is the acknowledgement of the perfect soul beyond what the physical body may show. That is beyond skin color, beyond sexual orientation, beyond cultural differences, and beyond any other characteristic which differentiates us from them.

We respect our bodies by eating the right foods and nourishing our minds with non-violent activities. Watching movies which depict cruelty, rape or torture or the disrespect of one person towards another, does not respect our Humanness. How can we have peace in our lives when we dwell on war, pain and cutting up people as our choice of entertainment? The same is true about the propaganda which is received by our minds feeding on media sources which are obviously bias against others.

Our in-dwelling Spirit naturally seeks peace. A child does not choose to cry if he or she can laugh. What would you prefer to do? If you do not choose to honor yourself with what is good in life, you may open yourself up to allowing someone else to make the choices for you – and they may choose a lifestyle which is not in your best interest. Again, it is YOUR choice. You CAN accept and receive peace, respect and love if you want it. And you may also accept an Interfaith atmosphere with all your brothers and sisters in the world.

## Step Three

*I accept and receive each person I meet as a child of God and honor them with peace, respect and love.*

Now, Step Three may be easier for most people than Step Two. Sometimes we want to be so helpful to others, we overlook ourselves. However, once we do choose to honor ourselves, we can find it that much easier to honor others who we meet with peace, respect and love. Imagine if everyone were to do that!

World Peace will begin when people are willing to stop judging others solely by their appearance. Bigotry and discrimination must disappear and be replaced with acceptance. This is beginning to happen throughout our planet and needs to continue as a way of life for all people everywhere. Acceptance and Interfaith must become a way of life.

When we accept ourselves as a child of God we cannot exclude any of our Brothers and Sisters no matter what color of skin they have chosen to wear. Short, tall, fat, skinny, old, young, no matter what – we are all the same inside with the same fragilities as the next person. We all want to be happy and we all want to be safe. With your help, we can all be at Peace which will extend to our families and friends and eventually those who we may one day meet.

## Step Four

*I forgive myself for past actions which hurt others.*

In order to create World Peace, we must more fully understand and develop a vital human quality which is called Forgiveness. I call Forgiveness a "stuffer" quality because when we are in a position to forgive our self or another person, we often give a superficial "I'm sorry" and then move on. We "stuff" the true depth of hurt we may be experiencing inwardly and act as if it is fully over even when we are still feeling the effects of the event. This is the experience we receive when we use the words "SHOULD HAVE" when speaking about our self. I should have taken that job I was offered. I should have married that other person. I should have taken better care of my body when I was younger. I should have voiced my unhappiness earlier in the relationship. How many past "should haves" do you use? How angry or unforgiving of yourself are you? And how many times have you said "I'll never forgive that so-in-so no matter how long I live"... how many?

Forgiveness is one of the miracle actions of life which has rewards far beyond what the forgiver feels he or she is giving the forgiveness for. Can you imagine the freedom a person might feel who, after being locked up in a cage for years, now has no limits as to where he can travel? The freedom and ability to move without being in bondage is what anyone who truly forgives can feel. Forgiveness breaks the tether, which is holding you from advancing in your career, your relationships, your health, your peacefulness. Forgiving is like unstopping a sink which is backed up. With a few pumps of the plunger, the clog is dislodged, and the water begins to flow again. Is your life flowing exactly the way you want it to? You may need to take a Personal Inventory.

Have you ever talked bad about a group of people who you really did not know? Have you lumped bad people of another faith into a, "They are all like that" category? I laugh in an unbelieving way when friends from other faiths tell me about some of the cruel misrepresentations people say about their faith. "They are all terrorists." "They all are rich with big noses and want to run the world." "All they do is sit around and make weird noises." Have you ever told someone about how bad a faith group was only to find out later that your source was bias? Did you go back and say, "I AM Sorry" to that person?

It is very important to take a personal inventory every now and then to make sure you are not acting prejudicial with people you interact with. A personal inventory is like an inventory taken of a store's merchandise; you list the good and the bad as you see it. Notice that I said to list the GOOD as well as the bad. There are probably more good things that we do than the bad. Unfortunately, we have a tendency to look only at what is "bad" in us when we do a personal inventory, and that is always just a very small percentage of our total make-up. Identify what you have done incorrectly and applaud yourself for what you do well.

If you have participated in the Fourth Step in another 12-Step program, and did a thorough job, you do not need to repeat it here. If however, you have not, now is the time. One thing to remember is, YOU ONLY HAVE TO DO IT ONCE! Once the inventory is complete, you only have to decide what needs to be released and what new inventory you may want to acquire to replace it. This could look like trading hate for love, illness for good health, war for peace, etc.

Remember, Step Four deals with forgiving yourself. As you slow down and give yourself a few hours to analyze your past, what is on your list of things which you have not forgiven yourself for? Forget minor occurrences. We all irritate people unknowingly each day. What are the things which spring to mind which you feel your actions hurt yourself or someone else? What old negative inventory are you holding onto? The fact is you cannot change the past. What happened in the past by your actions, happened! You cannot change those occurrences. You can only learn to identify them, and then release them through forgiving yourself for the occurrences. This acceptance of oneself just as you are, is the beginning of the letting go process which can bring about a more peaceful life. You need to accept yourself exactly as you are, then as you change you will have an even greater power to change.

## Step Five

*I forgive others for past actions which, I felt, hurt me.*

Step Five, like Step One, is another more difficult Step. It is forgiving others for past actions which, YOU FELT hurt you. The key words here are obviously "<u>you felt</u>." Have you ever apologized for saying something to someone only to find that the person didn't remember the incident? Just because we see an action as harmful, doesn't mean the other person feels the same way. Right now, you may be holding onto some words a parent said to you when you were a teenager which angered you. That parent may not even be aware of saying those words or how those words affected you. As a child you may have teased another child for whatever reason. Perhaps you went along with "the gang" to embarrass or hurt someone. Are you still angry at yourself for being pulled into the prank?

The work which is needed to be done in Step Five only needs to be done once. When Steps Four and Five are complete you let them go and release the experiences to God or your higher power. Of course, we have to do daily maintenance each day which we will cover later.

As with Step Four, we need to make a list of all people who we feel harmed us and who we need to forgive. Imagine how much energy we can gain for our own good by exchanging it for the old negative thoughts we are holding onto. We need to approach those people and tell them how we feel in a mature way. This might sound something like:

> *"Bob, I need to talk with you for a minute and I need you to be quiet while I say what I have to say. I don't know if you remember back in (whenever) when you said (whatever), but I want you to know that really hurt me. I felt (whatever) and, for whatever reason, I never said anything about it to you when it happened. I just wanted to let you know how I felt and that I forgive you for your words (or actions)."*

Now the truth is, it doesn't matter how Bob responds. The encounter was not done for Bob's sake. It was done for yours. If Bob defends his actions or apologizes saying "I had no idea how you felt," the holding on process is no longer in effect. You have released the negativity which was part of holding on to the event. Once you have done this for all of the MAJOR negative events you are tethered to, there are no limits how much Peace you can bring into your world.

Imagine someone who is bogged down with work (this may be you?). Imagine someone who juggles five or six projects at one time and tries to carry on a normal life. Now imagine that half of his or her work is no longer necessary. Can you FEEL the freedom? Imagine yourself having the free time to play, to smile, to be happy. This is what can happen when you no longer hold the actions of past events against past relationships. Now you are ready to move on.

# Step Six

*I am entirely ready to have God remove any defects of character which reduce the possibilities of Peace around me.*

Step Six is an easier step although completely necessary for our acceptance of Peace in our lives. Being "ready" indicates a willingness to let go – to let go of everything you found in Steps Four and Five. Do you still want to hold onto a few of those angry thoughts about someone who you felt harmed you? You have the mental right to be miserable too you know. What do YOU want? Step Six begins your new consciousness of being willing to have good come into your life. You become willing to be Peace-filled. You become willing to be tolerant and loving to all those you meet and to those who you may never meet. You become willing to become a friend to yourself and everyone around you, even to those who do not look or speak like you. Can you FEEL it? As you become willing to let go of all which does not bring Peace in your life, you begin to let go of wrong thinking or feelings which might have held you back. You begin to talk more nicely with yourself when you catch yourself doing something which before would have caused you distress. Let it all go in Love and it will come back to you in the same way. This is what Interfaith offers you.

# Step Seven

*I humbly ask God to remove any blockages within me to creating Peace around me.*

Okay, so you have examined yourself and identified blockages which existed in your past which you used to reduce the Peace you could have received. You are now aware of the problem area(s) and, by being aware, are now ready to remove them. However, Step Seven is directly linked to Step One. As strong as we have become as humans, the God-presence within us is stronger. So here we come to another "surrender" step. We humbly ask the stronger part of ourselves to remove any blockages which still exist so we can experience the full peace we deserve. And we are talking about peace in ALL area of your life. Even the ones of which you are fully aware.

The asking which we do is done humbly from the human part of us. God can do anything. We can't. So, doesn't it make sense to turn over our greatest challenges to the greatest Power in our lives? It's like trying to hold onto a handful of sand. The harder we try to hold it, the more sand filters through our fingers. When we approach the task gently with an open hand, more sand stays in our hand. In the same way when we admit "we need God within us to do the work", we have surrendered. And in that surrendering, we accept people who we are not fully acquainted with yet.

Be careful; our human side can be stubborn. We keep hearing the child voice within us seeking power and whining *"Daaadddd, I'd rather do it myself."* If you have done step seven for all of the MAJOR negative events which you might be tethered to, there are no limits how much Peace you can bring into your world. You may even free yourself to go to an Interfaith meeting in your community and bring new friends into your life.

## Step Eight

*I make a list of all people with whom I am not at peace, and become willing to make amends to them all.*

Now that you have completed the work on yourself, it is time to clean up any past relationships which are reducing the amount of Peace you are receiving in your life. For this Step you will be making a list of people and being willing to make amends to all of those whose lives you "think you have harmed." You only need to be "willing" to make amends at this point.

The emphasis is on the words "think you have harmed." These are NOT people to whom you said a few wrong words. These are people who were ACTUALLY HARMED by your actions or non-actions, meaning their lives were changed by you. It is unlikely you harmed more than a few people in your life to this degree and they were probably in your immediate family.

Make the list and be willing to make the amends.

## Step Nine

*I make direct amends to all people with whom I am not at peace.*

After you have made a list of all people with whom you are not at Peace, it is time to make direct amends to those people. This is done wherever possible EXCEPT WHEN TO DO SO WOULD INJURE THEM OR OTHERS. This humbling step of admitting error to those whom we have harmed, is a purifying action which has incredible healing power AFTER it is completed. I do not believe it is possible to explain to another person who has not gone through this Step, what a beautiful, cleansing action it is. Whether it is to a parent, a child, a relative or whatever, once this is done, years of upset will be purged from your mind.

The healing in this step comes from an honest and complete admitting of your wrongdoing(s) which caused you not to be at peace. The amends need to be done in person, briefly and without emotion. This might sound something like:

> *"Bob, I'd like to apologize for (words, actions, etc.) when we were working on (such-and-such project). I made a mistake and I would like to clear the air between us and admit my error. I hope you will accept my apologies."*

How would you feel if someone apologized to you in this way? It is important to be honest and frank, yet humble enough to realize the person may not want to accept your apology. That is on them. Your job is to make the offer and not beg them to forgive you. If they want to hold a grudge, it is their right and you have to permit them their decision. However, as you release the incidents which led up to the lack of Peace in this relationship, you no longer hold onto the negative energies of the experience. You are set free and you win! If the person accepts the apology, you also win. You cannot lose.

If you choose not to make your amends in person, or because the person you hurt is no longer alive or available, this process needs to be done during your prayer time. In as much detail as possible, see the amends being offered and then accepted by the other person. You might do this in a letter. See a completion! Do this step and move on! Feel the Peace enter your life and begin to find ways to assist others to receive the Peace they seek. You will not go un-rewarded.

## Step Ten

*I continue to take personal inventory and, when I cause a situation not to be peaceful, I promptly admit it.*

We now come to what is referred to in 12-Step as the three "maintenance steps." After the past is cleaned up, we STOP LOOKING BACKWARDS and begin looking to the present. We want Peace now and we begin to focus on the individual strengths it takes to have Peace in our lives on a daily basis.

Because you are no longer bogged down by your past, you are free to develop those loving peace-filled qualities you have always desired. What begins to make all of this possible in our minds is, other people around this planet are going through the same process we are. We understand no matter what country, culture, conditions, etc. a person comes from or lives in, we and they are the same. Skin color means nothing. Income bracket means nothing. Sexual orientation does not matter. We recognize that everyone we meet wants what we want; we are only here for Peace.

In Step Ten we become a visitor from another planet standing next to ourselves and observing our behavior. Each moment we watch ourselves and become aware of how we express Peace in our daily lives. We develop a sense of humor when peaceful things do not occur. We catch ourselves in the middle of a sentence in which we have expressed an un-peaceful thought and we negate the statement and affirm "Peace is here now." We also check ourselves when we meet others who are not "like us." What can we learn from their differences? How can we improve our lives by letting Interfaith be at the hub of our being?

As we promptly admit our wrong thoughts or actions to ourselves during the day, we are brought to a new peaceful consciousness which makes it easier to see and do Peace in the future. Every peaceful activity begins a chain-reaction with others who are affected by our actions. As we all begin to flow with the peaceful God-presence within us, we begin to realize "All things are Possible with God." That includes World Peace!

## Step Eleven

*I seek through prayer and meditation to improve my conscious contact with God as I understand God, praying only for knowledge of God's peaceful will for me and the power to carry it out.*

Step Eleven is easy for most people once they get into the habit of doing it. Like exercising in the morning, eating healthy food, not surrounding yourself with violent entertainment or company, once we get into HEALTHY habits, things begin to flow positively for us. Interfaith becomes the new normal.

It is interesting to hear the words coming out of a doctor's mouth when a patient has been discovered to have a serious illness. After all the medical procedures have been done the comment most heard is "all we can do now is pray." Why do we wait until the end to pray? Why not make it part of our daily life now? So, how do we start? Believe it or not, it is relatively easy.

"I seek through prayer and meditation" is a present tense affirmation stating, "I am in the process." I am doing it – now! As a seeker, we look for those processes which will benefit our lives. We become "open" to new ideas and welcome inspiration which brings us new understandings. We seek to find! "We seek to find" sounds simple but it has deeper meaning. As children playing a hide and seek game, the fun was in the "finding" as much as in the hiding. With enthusiasm we sought out other children or hidden objects. The action of seeking stirred up our energy and we probably let out a loud shriek when we finally found the person or object we were looking for. Think back. Can you remember the anticipation as you opened a special gift from someone you loved? Maybe your heart raced a little and your breath became full. And when you opened the gift and saw the joy which had been bestowed upon you by a loved one, perhaps your eyes were filled with tears. Remember the emotion?

### *Imagine finding World Peace.*

We seek World Peace and Inner-Peace through daily prayer and meditation. By creating the habit of spending time each day stopping, thinking, and knowing the good is happening in and all around us, we become focused on making it happen. It doesn't matter which form of meditation you do. The outer form means nothing. It is the inner thinking which does the work. There is a chapter on the process of meditation later in this book.

So why do we pray and meditate – "to improve our conscious contact with God as we understand God." Peace is not the reason we pray. Peace is the result we experience once we improve our contact with the higher presence within us. It doesn't matter what "name" you give to God, only that the higher presence is acknowledged and daily sought after for support and love. God has to work for you in order to improve your life. Remember, we cannot create Peace by ourselves. We need each person establishing a conscious contact with the God-presence (TRUTH) within them and then directing all that loving presence out to the world. Imagine seeing God in the eyes of everyone you meet, no matter what faith they belong to or if they do not belong to any faith.

The last part of Step Eleven is another surrender – "praying only for knowledge of God's peaceful will for me." Many of us were brought up with the understanding that prayer was used to convince God, if we begged loud enough, what God should give us in our life. This of course presumes we know more than God – not a good assumption! As many times as I had wished a certain direction to be true for me at that moment, I learned God had other ideas and even better directions for my life. So, instead of beseeching God for the results I seek, I have learned to let go and ask for God's guidance for everyone's highest good. In my daily prayer time I state "God, you know what I need in order to help bring Peace on Earth and I ask that those people, circumstances and conditions are brought into my life in divine time for the good of all concerned. When I ask for something, I always follow it up with, "This or something better."

The letting go process allows for God to bring us much more than our limited human self-desires. When I had first envisioned INTERFAITH in 2005, it did not have the breadth or scope of the project which is before me today. Thank you God for placing no limits to the possibilities.

Finally in Step Eleven we end with a humble request "for the power to carry out God's will." We pray for the faith, guidance, physical, emotional and mental strength, and ability to carry out God's plan for us and those around us. And it is so!

## Step Twelve

*Having had a change in consciousness as a result of these steps, I choose to carry the message of Peace to others and to practice these principles in all my affairs.*

In Step Twelve we acknowledge we have developed a changed consciousness, had a spiritual awakening, are born-again, whatever you wish to call it and, because of this, we choose to carry the message of Peace to ALL others and practice it every day. The operative words are CHOOSE and PRACTICE.

We need to CHOOSE Peace in order to have it. We need to PRACTICE it in all we do. Peace must become part of us our lives; the way we think, the way we go through our day, the way we interact with our family, the way we treat our boss and co-workers the way we speak to a waitress or cab driver, the way we lovingly treat other drivers on our roads and freeway systems. We must BE Peace with ALL people. Are there people at work who are from a faith different than yours? Make it a point to sit down with them and show them that you are interested in how and what they think.

If we want the 12-Steps to work for us we have to work them. The power comes from repeat working and repeat surrendering and then watching our Peace manifest.

Now that we have created peace within ourselves and have become open to Interfaith happening in our lives, we need to develop places for the good to happen. Places can be created where world peace can develop and interfaith can happen on a larger scale. My suggestion is to create TALK ZONES in our communities. These may help us increase our understanding of Interfaith and PEOPLEism™.

# TALK ZONES ™

So what are TALK ZONES?
   TALK ZONES are answers to help reduce loneliness through people's brief encounters with one another. They are perfect places for Interfaith groups to meet and discuss business and or current affairs. TALK ZONES are physical places in which we can walk up to someone and, without fear, feel comfortable to begin a meaningful conversation. The phrase 'TALK ZONE' gives us permission to speak to and interact peacefully with strangers we would otherwise pass-by.

We experience different zones every day; speed zones which make us slow down, hospital zones which force us to be quiet and time zones which let us know when to place a call. We have no-parking zones, hard-hat zones, loading zones and no-smoking zones. So many zones, yet none created to bring people together for something good – for something peaceful which can offset the mistrust and isolation we may have created for ourselves. I call for each one of us to demand or create TALK ZONES in the environments we use.

I want every restaurant and coffee shop to have an area with a TALK ZONE sign permitting strangers to dine together and to talk with one another. I want every government building to have TALK ZONES so strangers who are waiting for services have a chance to meet each other. I want every religious building to have an area with a TALK ZONE sign which allows people to get to know each other even when services are not being held.

I do not want to sit in an airport again without seeing travelers from around the world communicating with each other in a TALK ZONE. This can be a conduit to help spread world peace. What about in your community? Could a non-threatening, caring, TALK ZONE be the place where a lonely teen can find someone to hear his or her story. Perhaps an elderly resident can find a friend or maybe a group of people can meet to set-up a neighborhood block party.

Think of the possibilities!

Loneliness might be eliminated! And the most beautiful thing about a TALK ZONE is, even when no one else is there, you can share the space and peace with God or Spirit or whatever you call your Higher Power. And even if you do not belong to a faith or spiritual community, perhaps a TALK ZONE can reduce any loneliness you might be experiencing.

The best part about TALK ZONES are their simplicity. There are no rules, structures nor special designs other than a TZ Sign. TALK ZONES work because they can be created by children, ministers, community leaders, mayors, heads of countries... by you! A 'TALK ZONE' sign can be crayoned on a sheet of paper and taped to a wall. It can be carved in stone in the middle of a community park. There are no limits to where a TALK ZONE can be created and where PEOPLEism can be implemented.

I define my TALK ZONE sign as the one below. My greatest prayer is that when you see this trademarked sign, no matter where you are in the world, you will be welcomed and befriended by all who are within the space. Possible locations for a TZ are described on the next pages.

## ABUSIVE TZers

Let us be realistic. There are some people who, after they begin to speak, we realize we want nothing to do with them nor their conversation. They are "Takers." What the world needs more of is "Givers." If a "Taker" comes into a TALK ZONE you are visiting, I suggest you handle the situation in the following way. Be honest and tell the person you are not interested in their topic and thank them for sharing. Either begin a new subject with them, start a conversation with someone else, or go find another TALK ZONE in the neighborhood.

Because someone is sad or lonely, has an inflated ego, whatever, and needs to talk, does not give them the right to "dump" all of their troubles in your lap. If you feel you can and want to help them in some way, even by just listening, then do so. Otherwise, walk away politely and mentally encircle that person in a white light of healing and know you are both better for meeting. Your job is not to heal other people but to "see them healed" through their own inner God-presence.

Note: You may be experiencing a talkative "Taker" person because you need to learn the art of listening and "Giving." Now let's look at some applications of creating TALK ZONES in environments we use every day.

# TALK ZONES LOCATIONS

## TZs In Restaurants

Imagine being alone for lunch or dinner. You may be in a strange city or just refuse to cook a meal in your own kitchen. Most people avoid fancy restaurants when they are by themselves because they feel uncomfortable sitting alone at a table set for a larger party. There is also the stigma of 'not having a date'.

I was standing in line at a St. Louis English Pub dinner theater one evening knowing the atmosphere was designed to be fun and a little risqué. The hostess was dressed in English 'wench' clothing and was cleverly joking with the people who reached the front of the line.

"So deary" she said to a gentleman, "how many in your party?" When he replied "just one", she loudly announced to the dining hall, "By yourself! Oh you poor dear. Couldn't get a date?" Everyone laughed including the customer. When my date and I reached the head of the line and told her there were two in our party, the hostess loudly announced, "another couple who have no friends." In that environment it was okay to be alone. In other restaurants you might find yourself at a small table near the back door. In a TALK ZONE you will be lonely only if you choose to be.

Each time I visit a hotel restaurant during a business trip, I look at the business travelers who are seated at the dining tables. On a long bench seat, there is usually exactly one table between each person and the next traveler dining alone. It usually looks like a picket fence with each traveler's face looking more bored than the next. Some people want their privacy which is okay. We each require our own space now and then. But why do people who want to meet and talk with others have to suffer? This will be especially true as you get more involved in Interfaith.

Imagine walking into a restaurant in a strange city and the waiter asking you if you would like: "Smoking, Non-Smoking or a TALK ZONE." All TALK ZONES are non-smoking. As you enter the TALK ZONE area you would be seated with strangers at a large round table whose occupants would extend their hands and welcome you. Names would be exchanged, and you would join in the conversation. You then become part of a new family – you would become a 'TZ'er!

Restaurants are ideal for TALK ZONE areas due to the seating flexibility most dining establishments have with booths and tables. An entire room or just a corner of one area could be set up as a TZ at first and then allowed to expand as the interest increases. Once a restaurant becomes known as a place to come to meet and talk with new people, it might become a regular place-to-meet for interesting people.

TALK ZONES are not like "pick-up" bars. The object is not to meet people who you might want to spend the night with or marry one day, although nothing is impossible. TZs are places to visit when you need a friend or just want some conversation revolving around peace or interfaith. Imagine all of the smiling faces you will have the possibility of creating just by your visit.

Eating places around the country are used for business net-working meetings, self-help groups and organizations, athletic committee meetings, as well as all types of social groups which attempt to attract new members. I am familiar with a number of restaurants which host one or two different meetings every weekday and some on the weekends. The difference between these activities and a TALK ZONE is, a TZ is not scheduled, does not have an agenda and has neither formal beginnings nor ends. It might have TZ information which the host establishment obtains from me. Otherwise … the activities depend upon who is sitting in the space. If you request to be seated at a TALK ZONE in a restaurant, you may end up talking with some people who are having dessert, some their main meal or others just a beverage. They may be a business traveler, a local merchant taking a break or a retired person looking for someone with whom to pass some time.

I believe all things happen for a reason and, if you end up talking with a person or people who make you feel uncomfortable, you may want to ask yourself "what do I have to learn from this situation?" It may be tolerance, patience, or maybe it is a chance for you to speak up for yourself and say "thank you for sharing" and then leave the table. Who knows, you might meet someone who wants to put a million dollars in your new business venture or has the ultimate recipe for carrot cake or a faith's cultural dish. All things are possible when we center ourselves on Love and Peace.

When a friend of mine heard of my TALK ZONE dreams, she suggested I contact a major coffee house chain and ask them to dedicate a TZ spot in each of their locations. Great Idea! Where would you like to see a TALK ZONE?

## TZs In Business

From the early 1980s to the mid-1990s I spent much of my time on airplanes and in rental cars going from state to state helping business owners open their new retail locations which I had designed. Along with doing the corporate work, I was separately delivering business seminars to corporate executives, small business owners and the United States Navy. Throughout the mid-90s into today, my corporate business training became supplemented by my spiritual work and the deep belief that God is a loving God and wants me, and everyone else, to succeed beyond our human expectations. Once I began combining spirituality with business, all of the pieces of my life came together that much more quickly and that much more perfectly. Then in 2000 I wrote the book TALK ZONES and in 2005 began my work with Interfaith.

Aside from the hours we spend at home with the people we love and who love us, not to mention the time the hours we spend sleeping, our lives are full of the work we have chosen to do in the business we have chosen to work in. Working "nine to five" has always been a myth and it is not unusual for most people to spend much more than forty hours per week at the office. The higher we move up the corporate ladder, the more time we spend at our jobs. And if someone should choose to open his or her own business, it is not unusual for them to spend half their life at the office or doing office-related business from home.

The business environment is crying out for TALK ZONES. Brian J. Grim, Ph. D., is president of the Religious Freedom & Business Foundation (RFBF) and a leading expert on how faith and business build a better world. Brian's research reported that "religion contributes $1.2 trillion to the U.S. economy annually, more than the combined revenues of the top 10 technology U.S. companies including Apple, Amazon and Google." A typical "worker" at all ends of the employee spectrum, need a place to "take a break" and, when necessary, have a place where they can discuss life issues with other people. This is essential for good mental health. And it is essential for each worker to meet and interact with other company workers from all faiths who have a part in the growth of their company.

Creating a TZ as part of the break room or by itself in a "common room" can open up the chance for employees to learn more about each other and perhaps get greater outside insight into projects they are working on. It can bring about a greater "family" atmosphere in an otherwise driven environment. And those friendships which will be created at work can spill over to more social and outside activities. It is a win-win for all.

## TZs At Worship

Another ideal place to add a TALK ZONE is in or around the thousands of churches, synagogues, mosques and other spiritual spaces which exist throughout the world. Many people go to church to receive spiritual guidance from the priest, minister. imam or rabbi who is conducting the service. Many times, they are also looking for new friendships and perhaps an outlet to vent certain frustrations. However, when the service is over and people leave, the opportunities for guidance also usually ends.

Most churches do not have space within their sanctuary for a TZ and, if they did, a conversation might bother other people who are praying or meditating. If a separate room is not available, imagine a TZ sign mounted on a wall near the entrance of the church with chairs positioned in a circle near it. The area does not have to be large but should have room enough if others want to participate in a discussion.

Many religious groups have coffee and cookies available for people after the services. This is a perfect time to have a TZ available for first-time attendees so other church officials could recognize newcomers who might want to talk. The worst mistake a house of worship could make is to ignore a new congregate. Everyone is a potential link to World Peace.

As with all TZs, any peaceful topic may be appropriate for discussion even though the location is in a church. It could be exciting to learn that people, or a person you have seen at services for some time but have not talked to, has the same interests as you outside the church. You might even develop a new best friend! Spirituality can be experienced in many ways.

I also believe the PURPOSE of all religious centers is to be spiritually driven to create peace on earth. Whether you study Hinduism, Buddhism, Confucianism, Taoism, Judaism, Islam, Christianity, or any organized religion's beliefs, aside from those groups which preach hatred, "Love" is at the center of their belief. For many there is an acknowledgement of the inherent presence of the divine in every being, some in everything. Unfortunately, too many lives have been lost in war over which religion is the "right one." When we are concerned only on the rituals of any religion, we move away from the beauty and spirituality of the belief. As we mature as humans, hopefully we will be able to talk with each other to reduce the separateness we may sometimes feel around new people.

I have been blessed to have traveled extensively. When I meet people of different cultures, I am amazed at how similar we are to one another. The old saying of 'if we had to fight each war naked, there would be no wars' is probably very true. Once we meet our "enemy" we find out, for the most part, they value the same things we do. They want to be happy, they have families and dreams and, inwardly, they seek peace. We learn this only when we get the chance to talk with them. Maybe their symbols of religion are different from ours but their spirituality is the same. Each religion begins to look the same if we consider them to be the many spokes on a wheel. As we approach the hub from the outside, each spoke gets closer and closer. The hub is whatever we call God. Now we just need a TALK ZONE to give us permission to discuss this further.

## TZs In Airports

An airport can be a lonely place for a traveler who is waiting between planes. Boarding areas are perfect places for TALK ZONES. If you have travelled and have make a point of speaking with strangers, you have probably encountered some unexpected wonderful conversations over the years. I know I have. I have met people from around the world and have learned things from them which I am able to refer to later in conversations with other people. However, most airport seating areas have been designed for the efficiency of people and baggage movement... not for conversation. Yet there are usually smaller seating areas near most airport gates which have seats facing other seats. These areas are perfect to hang a double-sided TALK ZONE sign over. Imagine not having to sit alone bored for an hour or being forced, out of boredom, to purchase a ten-dollar hot dog and drink. Consider the chance to network with other travelers and share your experiences and expertise. You may find it so enjoyable you might want to visit your own city's airport when you are not traveling just to be in a TALK ZONE.

The publicity for the airlines should be enough to offset the very low cost of purchasing and installing a TALK ZONE signs over existing seating areas by the gates. An airline which offers a place for international travelers to talk with one another and communicate their human feelings, would be perceived of as a company interested in world peace. Imagine seeing "United for Peace" at TALK ZONES at every United Airlines boarding gate?

# TZs In Health Care Facilities

One of the most boring and sometimes depressing things you can do is to accompany someone to a health check-up and have to wait in the building lobby or office waiting room while they are being examined. These places can be anything but peaceful.

I remember sitting in a doctor's waiting room along with nine or ten other people who were waiting to be examined or waiting for someone else. Each person hid behind a magazine which they strategically positioned in front of their face. No one looked at anyone else in the room for fear of intruding on the other's privacy. Suddenly the front door opened and a young woman with an 18-month old child entered the room. Within moment after the mother was seated, the child had befriended everyone in the room. People were smiling and talking, and although the conversation had begun with baby topics, it was not long before all types of things were being discussed. A TALK ZONE had been accidentally (?) created by a child.

There are many ways to make a quiet waiting room come alive. I have been to some doctor's offices which had checker boards and backgammon sets out on small tables in the center of the room. I remember one doctor's office which had brightly colored, optical illusion prints on the walls of the waiting room. Other offices I have visited have had unusual artwork or funny posters on the walls. Each attempt like this reduces tensions for visitors and, without trying, creates a TALK ZONE.

If we ever need a sense of peace, it is at the doctor's office. Studies have been done which show people who receive loving attention during an illness, recuperate faster than those who are left alone. We need others! Even if you enjoy alone time as most people do, contact with others is healthy for our human organism. If you think about it, many counselors, therapists, social workers, psychologists, etc., help to make others "well" by listening to them. Have you ever felt better after a long talk with your best friend? See! Imagine having best friends and being a best friend to people all around the world.

It Is Possible!

# TZs In Shopping Malls

Neighborhood shopping malls are easy places in which to create TALK ZONES. Although most malls are designed with conversation and meeting areas in them, many are not designed with seating close enough together and facing other seating to be used as a TZ. This can be easily changed by adding another row of individual chairs or fixed pedestals between or among the existing seating.

Since the first enclosed shopping mall was built in 1955, shopping malls have become community gathering spots and used for various social activities. This, however, is usually done on large scale activities such as music concerts, exercise demonstrations or 4-H club type fairs. With good TZ signs located around these activities, each mall can become energized with small group discussion areas which could stimulate new friendships and healings. Retailers would love the additional activity since they realize the longer people stay near their store, the greater the chance there is for someone to buy something.

Supermarket owners could increase their revenues by creating a TALK ZONE at the front of their stores. Shoppers could talk about peace, their future and possibly the food specials they found throughout the store. One supermarket near me sells cups of gourmet coffee near the store entrance. Unfortunately, there is no place to sit down with the coffee so you cannot take a moment to talk with other shoppers. Here is another TZ opportunity!

While I was writing the original TALK ZONE article in 1990, I looked out of the window of the apartment I was renting at the time and saw a young woman obviously lost in the maze of apartments. When I asked if I could help, she asked me if I knew where Janice Somethingorother lived. I had no idea. Then I realized God was showing me a need. In that apartment complex of over 500 units, I did not know anybody by name. I knew where my next TALK ZONE would go. Where will you put yours?

# Supplemental Materials

Don't be surprised that the discussion in this Supplemental Materials section seems to have migrated from Interfaith to Communications. It is because until you know how to communicate effectively with people who you are familiar with, communications with someone who seems to be a stranger would be many times more difficult. But remember, this is the same issue when two Christians are talking together, two Buddhists, two Muslims, two Jews, etc. We must understand the basic structure of how to communicate effectively no matter who we are speaking with. This includes all of our friends and family in ANY social or business situation.

## 3 Steps to REBOOT Personal Peace

### Step One - Watch Your Words

Have you ever noticed even if you innocently say something to someone in jest, as non-aggressive as you may have meant it to be, it can be the impetus to almost start a war? I believe most people take for granted the area of communication and end up in positions where they have to apologize and have to use words similar to, "I was only joking!" Have you ever had to do that with family or people you grew up with? Not Peaceful Huh? Imagine how that lack of peace would be multiplied if the other person was a stranger from another faith!

Having poor communication skills can be very disturbing and devastating resulting in endless dollars lost in sensitive business situations. This has begun to be even more the case since much of our business communications comes from sending Emails back and forth. In many companies today the employees are encouraged not to stand up and go over to talk to another employee but, instead, send them an email. I believe e-mails can destroy business relationships and, on the other hand when used properly, can be a factor in the survival of a company. Short tweets of incomplete words are worse.

Experiments have shown when we communicate only with words such as reading an email or a letter, only 8% of the complete message the sender wants to get across is actually received on the other end. If the sender was to call and talk to the person so the receiver could hear his or her voice, only another 37% of the intended message would get through. The other 55% of a message needs to be delivered in-person through body language so the receiver can "experience" the intensity of the sender's message through the use of all the senses. The following exercise will help you understand why we need to realize the importance of **REBOOTING** this area for all our relationships. Read the next seven lines OUT LOUD. Each line has the same words yet each has a different word emphasized in the line. Listen to how each line sounds as you EMPHASIZE the underlined word.

<u>**I**</u> Never Told You To Do That
I <u>**NEVER**</u> Told You To Do That
I Never <u>**TOLD**</u> You To Do That
I Never Told <u>**YOU**</u> To Do That
I Never Told You <u>**TO**</u> Do That
I Never Told You To <u>**DO**</u> That
I Never Told You To Do <u>**THAT**</u>

Can you hear the difference? The words are the same but the emphasis is MUCH different. Imagine your boss emailing you something similar which ends with the phrase "do it now." Does "do it now" mean drop the priority project he gave you an hour before? Should it come before everything else on your plate including all of the fires you are putting out in your department? If you do not pick up the email because you are dealing with an emergency, will you still have a job tomorrow? Until you have a more complete understanding of the person's reason for sending the communication, you MAY NOT get the message which the sender is trying to relay. It is always the sender's responsibility to get the message across in an instantly understandable way.

The communication cycle must also be fully understood by all who are involved with getting a task done in order to get that task completed without extra cost to the company or the individual. Proper communications become that much more important when you are involved with people from a faith other than yours. This can be a task within a company or community with children of various ages or other adults as well as in a company with employees, managers or executive people who have a variety of backgrounds. When Person "A" sends a verbal communication to Person "B," is that communication? (This is not a test – it is simply me trying to present an important concept to you in a manner in which you may only understand 8% of my message.)

Person "A" ASSUMES when the words leave his mouth, Person "B" hears it the way Person "A" meant it to be heard. Have you ever said something to someone and then they turned around and said, "What? Sorry, what did you say?" It is possible when you spoke, the other person had his attention in another area. Is this ever you? – "Yeh Boss, I am listening, (and your mind says: pick up the shirts at the cleaners). Yes sir, go on, (mind says: buy milk and bread on the way home). Oh yeh, sure sir (mind says: pay phone bill before 5:00 pm)." Have you ever had to apologize to your boss for not getting a project done right the first time?

COMMUNICATION ONLY HAPPENS WHEN A MESSAGE IS TRANSMITTED, RECEIVED BY ANOTHER AND THE ONE SENDING THE MESSAGE GETS FEEDBACK FROM THE OTHER PERSON ACKNOWLEDGING WHAT HE OR SHE HEARD.

Without feedback you can never know if the receiver REALLY understood the message you gave him, especially when it is regarding an important item which must be handled in a timely manner. A wife asking her husband to pick up the kids from the movies at five o'clock when he is thoroughly engaged in watching a football game on television at three o'clock, may not be communicating effectively by hearing him reply by saying, "Uh Huh." Later, she could be very upset when she realizes the kids are still at the mall and dinner is ready to go on the table. Peace? No way!!!

One of the most peace-giving words in the English language is the word "YET." It can reduce the negative impact YOUR negative talk has on <u>YOU</u>. If you have a habit of saying things like, "I am not good at (whatever)," you need to **REBOOT** your self-talk. How peaceful can you be if all you hear from yourself are words describing how you are not good enough? If you want to degrade yourself, at least add the word "<u>YET</u>" after what you believe you are not good at. By saying "I am not a good listener <u>YET</u>," it puts some hope in your own mind <u>you will be</u> a good listener one day. "I am not the greatest computer user YET." I am not the best speaker YET." Hear it? Who knows, you may even get to appreciate your personal beauty as you **REBOOT** you!

If it is not obvious to you YET, good communications is not always an easy task. Without trying, feelings can be hurt and relationships ruined. Too many times when we do something wrongly, we mumble under our breath to the other person, "I'm sorry." I would like to suggest using the more emphatic "I <u>AM</u> SORRY!" when you find yourself in a communication quandary. "I <u>AM</u> SORRY for mishearing and/or misunderstanding what you actually wanted me to do." I <u>AM</u> SORRY for not fully communicating to you about how I felt about the situation." "I <u>AM</u> SORRY for not realizing I didn't get all the information from you before I started the project." Instead of blaming another or running through a list of irrelevant facts which does not help the peace of the situation, apologize for the miscommunication EVEN IF YOU WERE NOT TO BLAME. You may find it can mean the difference between going to war with another and possibly healing a much-needed relationship. This will be especially effective when you are attempting to communicate with someone from a different faith who has an accent which you find difficult to understand.

However, how can you apologize to someone who causes you NOT to be in peace? I believe people who constantly aggravate others, need to be Loved. They are crying out in their anger because they do not love themselves and want to feel superior. They do not like the way the world is changing around them and they do not like being out of control. Those who try to put us down, do so because they want to feel superior.

My wife and I have an acquaintance from another faith who used to be our friend. We served on committees together and did some good Interfaith work. Then for some reason which we do not understand, she began to say untruths about us even to our friends. Our friends have backed away from her due to her putting us down and being hard to deal with in general. If we end up in the same room as she, she will never even make eye contact with us. Her husband is just the opposite; he will come from across the room to make sure that we hug and speak together. I tell you this to let you know that I accept the fact that NOT EVERYONE will be your friend no matter how well you communicate. When we exhibit Love, peace and understanding WITHOUT ALLOWING OTHERS TO WALK OVER US, we have a better chance of **REBOOTING** into the peaceful communications WHICH people from any faith group seek.

**Step Two - Ask Clarifying Questions**
Mastering the art of asking clarifying questions can be one of the most important abilities a communicator who wants to live in peace can learn. When speaking or writing to anyone from any faith: a spouse, child, new hire or an employee who has not performed up to par or to someone with whom your vital information must be followed, asking them to orally repeat or put in writing the instructions you have given is of the utmost importance. If you find yourself in such a situation, and not wanting to sound like a parent speaking

to a disobedient child, you may want to phrase your statement in this manner; *"John, getting this project done right the first time is of the utmost importance to this company AND TO ME PERSONALLY. So that I can sleep tonight, and so that I will not have to answer to the Vice President tomorrow, please repeat back to me the instructions I just gave you so we know there are no misunderstandings."* By letting John know this is a very important issue which you are handing to him, he should be more than willing to repeat your directions. Do not be surprised if you have to modify what John believes he heard you say to what you actually said. This can be a great communication tool for both of you.

Questioning is vitally important when dealing with children and teenagers; doing it in the wrong way can limit your power and reduce their personal effectiveness with others as they grow up. Getting the answers to questions like, "Where are you going?" "Whom will you be with?" "At what number will I be able to reach you?" and "When will you be home?" can make any parent a little less worried or stressed. We want our kids to be independent; yet we are not at peace when they are not in our sight. **REBOOT** their thinking! Explaining why we are asking our questions to children is similar to getting someone at work to repeat our instructions back to us. They have to know our questions are not meant to control but to protect and make us peaceful. Telling them, "I am not asking these questions for you, I am asking them for me," helps them understand you have a stake in what happens to them. Unfortunately, they cannot fully understand your need for questioning until they have children of their own. We want to eliminate using the parent's curse of yelling, "When you have children, I hope they treat you just like you are treating me." Parents of children in all faiths, use that curse! What if we change that to, the "PARENT'S DREAM" and say exactly the same words in a proud, relaxed tone.

### NEVER ASSUME! NEVER ASSUME! NEVER ASSUME! ASK THE QUESTION!

If you were to believe the outcome of doing everything in your life correctly was critically important, would you not take all precautions to make sure those things would be done correctly? Of course you would! Others do not feel that way about YOUR things. They do about THEIR things, but not your things. We need to realize each person is doing what he or she feels would be right for them, so they can reach the goals they seek. When we assign a task to someone else, we have to realize they do not have as much invested in the outcome as we do. We cannot assume that everyone else understands what we understand.

When a young child breaks an expensive item while playing in the house, he has no understanding of the value of money. He hears you screaming at him and he knows he has done something wrong, yet his comprehension is not equal to yours. What does breaking the lamp mean? Especially when the next day you just replace it with a new one. The child cannot appreciate how much the lamp cost, how long it took you to earn the money to buy it, what amount of time it took from your other tasks to go and buy a new lamp and so on. Until it is their money and their time, the situation is never fully appreciated.

So it is with people at work who you assign a task to. If they were you, the task would be done correctly. THEY ARE NOT YOU! To make sure the job is done right we need to be asking the qualifying questions, which will make us peaceful enough to walk away and know the job will be done correctly the first time. Don't assume they completely understand the full range of the job unless you have seen them do it right at least once before. And if something has changed slightly, a procedure has been added, altered or eliminated, be sure they are aware of it. Doing these things will allow you to **REBOOT** and sleep peaceful throughout the night.

### Step Three - Know Yours & Other's Needs
Not only do people have different learning styles, people have different personality styles. If we can quickly identify those differences

in people and at the same time understand our own personality traits, we are well on our way to befriending everyone who we work or come in contact with. This is true no matter what a person's faith or cultural background is. Since there are twenty-six or more different personality programs in the United States today, let me discuss the four personality styles in an easy-to-use manner which you can understand and put into use immediately at work, home and in your social lives.

The chart on the next page, gives us the basics for the types of people we will meet in our everyday work life and whose types exist in any faith throughout the world. It is based on the fact that people are to some degree more AGGRESSIVE in their approach to others while other are less aggressive. Some people are more RESPONSIVE when people come up to them and others are less responsive. It is very important to understand each person is fine just the way he or she is and his or her personality differences are vital to producing a good working relationship. In fact, a team made up of people with only one type of personality is almost always doomed for failure or, at least, will do a lot more work to create a great final product than a team with well-balanced personalities.

The entertainment industry has known for a long time, a good balance of character types in a movie or television show will make or break the show. For me, the best and easiest example of this is with the very successful TV show and movie STAR TREK. (Note: If you do not remember the TV show Star Trek, you can easily exchange the four main characters from any successful TV show or movie. For example, with the main characters in the movie Harry Potter, Harry would be the Boss/Driver/Leader style, Hermione the Techie/Analytical/One-With-A-Plan style, Hagrid the Pleaser/ Amiable/Helper style and Ron the more Talkative/Worrisome/ Expressive style.) If you have any other favorite TV program or movie, identify the four major characters and they will optimize the four styles below.

(low)

| I.T. / Accounting. | R | CEO / Management |
|---|---|---|
| **Analytical** | E | **Driver** |
| | S | |
| Shy Body Movement | P | No Body Movement |
| Loves Details & Research | | Makes Final Decisions |
| Avoids People if Possible | O | Wants Bottom-Line Answers |
| Answers Take Time | | No-Frills in Discussion |
| | N | |

(low) A    G    G    R    E    S    S    I    V    E    N    E    S    S (high)

| H.R. / Counseling | I | SALES / P.R. |
|---|---|---|
| | V | |
| **Amiable** | E | **Expressive** |
| | N | |
| Friendly Body Movement | | Lots of Body Movement |
| Needs to HELP | E | Needs To Have An Audience |
| Wants EVERYONE to win | | Can "SELL" Almost Anything |
| Can Be Co-dependant | S | Has to Have a Voice |
| | S | |

(high)

Whether in the movies or on television, in Star Trek, Captain Kirk was the Driver/Boss style and always had the vision for the mission. He wanted bottom-line information to get his job done and was only in stress when his position was threatened by an alien or situation which tried to take his ship or overcome his power. This Driver style usually has little body movement when responding to others, stares directly at you while talking and, in a business setting, has the power to hire and fire. These Driver people plan out strategy for the company yet leave the details for others to complete. In the home, this could be the partner who wants to impose his or her will on the others by stating bottom-line reasons why such-and-such is the best course of action. They may be right! However, the method a Driver uses to get the message across can many times be intimidating. Most Kirk-like bosses use their short, concise and direct style of communicating to TELL people what they should or should not do. They have few people skills and rarely engage in "unneeded" discussion. This type of personality exists in EVERY Faith around the world. Sound like anyone you know?

Dr. Spock epitomizes the perfect Techie/Analytical Style person desiring only facts and logic preferring to spend time in research and not interact with people. His style is to avoid people who are irrelevant to his task and assist others with the data he collects. The body style for most analytical people is shy and they rarely have eye-to-eye contact with others. Unless specified by the person the Analytical is working for, time has no meaning for them; and a project is always an on-going adventure. In the home, this could be the partner who when you suggest a vacation, leaves the room and doesn't come back for days until EVERY possible vacation spot is researched thoroughly. When they feel comfortable with someone, they can talk on and on about the minute details of every aspect of an item or situation. When uncomfortable they blend into the background. Again, this type of personality exists in EVERY faith. Does this bring to mind anyone you know?

Scotty, the Chief Engineer on the Starship Enterprise, had the People-Pleaser/Amiable style in the program, always wanting to help and to be there when the ship needed more speed, warp drive or a crew member needed a friend to listen to his or her problem. His style can be associated with the family member or work associate who you can tell anything to and who is always there to assist. The personality loves to get to know people and to talk about friendly things usually starting with "I remember when …" Scotty's main conflict came when he helped too many people (being co-dependent) before himself and ended up feeling very stressed and overworked. In a home situation, this could be a partner who wants you and every other member to be happy first and goes to the trouble to fix your favorite foods, takes you out to dinner, fixes your broken whatever and is just a nice person. They have a difficult time deciding what THEY want and prefer to default to your preferences. An Amiable changes his or her mind very often and tries to make sure EVERYONE ELSE is happy. This type of personality exists in EVERY faith. Does this sound like you?

The Partier/Expressive character was Doctor McCoy who was always over excited at whatever was happening; he talked and explained his position over and over again with great vigor. His style is "to be heard" and to be very effusive in his mannerisms. He loved to talk and to even over-talk a subject just to get everyone to realize the problems as he saw them. He helped people with his medical expertise, and he tended to give advice when it was not asked for. In a home or business situation this would be a partner who will tell you much more about a subject than you feel you need to know. He or she gets very excited about doing things and enjoys multi-tasking. In fact, if an Expressive is only working on one or two things at the same time, he is usually bored. This type of personality also exists in EVERY faith. Can you picture someone like this?

This program's BALANCED team of characters created one of the most functional families/teams in the entertainment industry. The show will always be popular not just because of its Sc-Fi theme but because the talented members of the cast were balanced and helped to make the characters come alive. If your family or business team functions well, who is the Driver? The Analytical? The Amiable? The Expressive?

I counseled a family years ago which had a seemingly unruly 5-year old daughter which made even day-to-day activities very difficult to complete. She was constantly receiving disciplinary notes from her teacher and was in daily discord with other children at school. The parents were exhausted trying to reign her in and reduce the stress in the house. Upon examination I learned that the mother was VERY Amiable, the father VERY Expressive and the girl's 7-year old brother was VERY Analytical. When the daughter was born, unknowingly, she took the only personality position left in the family – She became the Driver! As such, she told everyone what to do, and expected everyone to follow her directions. Her response to being told what to do were answered with LOUD, emphatic NO! If a direction did not come from her, she was not compliant. Solution – I taught the parents how to alter their personality and take back the power by becoming more Driver. It worked!

If you remember or not, the major conflict between these four characters in Star Trek (and in any other set of personalities on any show) was between Spock and McCoy, the VERY analytical and the VERY expressive. The same is true in the work world, the interfaith world or in relationships and life in general. Conflict comes when our personality opposes another's, and steps are not taken to understand or adapt ourselves to people who are not like us. Offering people who want to do research the chance to be physically away from others, will help create respect and friendship. Giving a talkative person a little time to act out, can set the stage to have them help you with your projects. Positioning people who want to help in situations where they have the chance to help, can only create a positive relationship between you and them. And lastly, when dealing with the "power" person, giving them ONLY the bottom-line information they ask for can mean the difference between getting fired or receiving a raise.

Conflict can also come when someone's personality is EXACTLY like ours, causing there to be a power struggle. Two Driver-Kirk personalities can be explosive and be the source of broken relationships in the home, on the company's Board of Directors or when people from different faiths are working on a new project. The question comes up, who is in control? Two Analytical-Spock personalities can create a quiet, non-responsive attitude between people in a marriage or working together in any work environment. The question which develops in the silence could be, does he like me? Two Amiable-Scotty personalities may never feel they are doing enough for the other because both people are trying to help the other get what he or she wants. The question in their mind might be, what more can I do? Two Expressive-McCoy personalities are also explosive with each person attempting to have control over the conversation and present their ideas. The question develops, when will it be my turn? None of these relationships are healthy.

Do you want to know how to experience peace with other people, especially with those who when you see them coming, you cringe and pray they don't see you? If you do, or if you just want to enhance the relationship you have with another person, identify in which category of personality YOU fall, and then do the same for the other person. Within seconds you will see the reason there is conflict and you can then choose to deal with them in a different way – a way THEY would like to be treated. Be sure to do this when you meet people from a different faith. Understand, your problem with someone may be due to having opposite personality styles and not that they are of a different faith than you. this can be worked out once you fully understand it.

For example, if you are a People-Pleaser/Amiable/Scotty-Type personality who likes people and is always wanting to help others, and you need to interact with an Analytical Spock-Type personality who would prefer to work alone or a Boss/Driver / Kirk-Type personality who does not have time for more than the bottom-line discussion, by understanding that their style differs from yours and it is NOT BECAUSE THEY DISLIKE YOU that they act that way, your attitude will change. You no longer have to be upset when they are not as friendly as you would like them to be. THEY CANNOT BE AS FRIENDLY AS YOU WOULD LIKE BECAUSE IT IS NOT IN THEM. Rather than trying to change them or lose sleep about how badly you have been treated, you can accept them as they are and bring peace to yourself. No matter of which faith you follow, the more you treat an Analytical person by leaving him or her alone and converse with the Driver personality using bottom-line sentences only, the more they will like you and the friendlier they will be to you.

**Drivers, Analyticals and Amiables**, if you want to have peace with an Expressive person, tell them you have only five minutes before you have another appointment and ask them how they are and what they are working on. Prepare to listen.

**Drivers, Amiables and Expressives**, if you want to have peace with an Analytical person, ask them to do some research for you. Be sure to tell them exactly when you need the results.

**Drivers, Analyticals and Expressives**, if you want peace with an Amiable person, ask them their opinion or to help you with almost anything.

**Analyticals, Amiables and Expressives**, if you want peace with a Driver, do not be flowery or long-winded when you speak with them. Avoid them if the issue is not VERY important.

**Everyone,** if you want peace with someone who has a personality style the same as yours, give them what YOU would want. Drivers, give another Driver power. Analyticals give another Analytical a research project to do. Amiables, give another Amiable the chance to help you. Expressives, be quiet and give another Expressive the chance to shine. AHHH, finally, we can all live in peace!

# REBOOT Peace In Your Community

So we have come to realize, people are different. They have different intelligences, make decisions in different ways and have had different experiences when working with other people. Those from different faiths also have cultural experiences which you could not know about unless you had studied those faiths. As members of a family they may have different goals and at different ages, they may be more rebellious than at others. When these 'different' people get together to perform a task it is called teamwork; yet getting those different people to come together for a final goal can sometimes take work. A community's City Council or Planning Commission may be effective or not, depending on how well they handle Teamwork.

Creating an effective team and the environment for a team to grow in whether it is in a home or at work or in your community, ALWAYS includes the people involved going through 4 stages of development. Each stage may be conquered in one minute or may take hours or days to resolve. In some cases, a team may not be able to resolve even simple issues if it is not balanced by having a variety of personalities on it. Can you imagine a Community Work Program headed by all Driver personalities? Everyone would have their own vision and no one would want to work on the details. By understanding that these stages WILL OCCUR in the development of any team, the individuals involved can be more prepared for what may seem like personal attacks on their decision-making capabilities. Using Bruce Tuckman's 1965 model, the stages, in the order they appear, are called: Forming, Storming, Norming, and Performing.

The first stage, **Forming,** (when the team forms), deals with creating an atmosphere of open communication and respect among the people involved. This implies that each person should have the opportunity to discuss his or her feelings about why the team is coming together and what the goals of the team are. Because people process information differently, it is not unusual for members of the team who have heard what their assignment is from the parent, boss or advisory panel, to have different interpretations about what the team is tasked with doing. Depending on each member's experience with similar projects, he or she may have specific ideas about how the development of the project should proceed. Whether or not everyone in the group agrees as to what must be done, the team eventually moves into stage two – Storming.

**Storming** is probably the most important stage of development because it deals with any conflict, which may have come out of the Forming process. This stage brings out emotions and fears of individuals and must be dealt with completely before the team can go any farther. THIS IS WHERE MOST POORLY BALANCED TEAMS FAIL; often there can be too much emotion involved in the outcome. Communicating with others WITHOUT emotions can be difficult when you feel strongly about a particular method of dealing with an issue. Therefore, when you are speaking to another member of your team it is suggested you use a two-step method of communication. First, ask the person who you are in discussion with, "What do you feel would be a reasonable way to resolve this matter?" The answer from the other person should come in the form of:

"**I FEEL** ____(blank)____ **ABOUT** ____(blank)____
**BECAUSE** ____(blank)____."

This "I FEEL" statement needs to be followed by silence. Some more expressive team members may want to follow the I FEEL statement with further discussion and explanation and, as we discovered earlier, this can alienate other less expressive personality styles. This method works well for teams with Interfaith backgrounds.

The third stage in the development of a team is called **Norming** in which the team sets agreeable terms for completing the project it is working on. If the Storming part has been done well, this stage will probably go easily and quickly. At times, the team may have to re-visit the Storming stage in order to resolve an issue and move forward. Toggling back and forth from Norming to Storming is not unusual. On a complex community project this may happen at each meeting. The fewer emotions brought up over an issue, the easier it will be to resolve and reach the more important overall goal. Expressive beware!

The last stage of development is called **Performing**. This is the stage in which the team actually does the work which it is tasked to do. In it is created the end-result of the team's efforts. Through this last stage, problems will occur. It is imperative the team use a system to quickly understand and settle any problem which comes up. The following "MEMORANDUM" form is the quickest way I have found to resolve ANY problem. Whether it is a problem with your teenager or the forming of an Interfaith team in your community, this form works to eliminate the problem. On ONE sheet of paper write the following:

### MEMORANDUM
**Date:**
**To:**
From:
**PROBLEM:** (State the problem in one (1) sentence.)

**BACKGROUND:** (Give the background of the problem in one paragraph = 3-4 sentences)

**RECOMMENDATION:** (Bullet one or two possible ways to solve the problem including the costs if applicable)

This one-page process has never failed me and is simple for even a child to use when confronted with a problem. First, state the problem in one sentence. This helps you define what the problem really is and defines the same for the decision maker you are planning to send it to. The background gives you and the reader a full understanding of why the problem exists in the first place. As a manager of the problem, it is your job to solve problems which is why the last line offering recommendations is necessary. You may find when you reach this line, you have already figured out what to do about the problem. Assuming you do not need special funding or approvals, this memorandum may never need to be sent. Since making your department or team or family work properly is part of YOUR job, a **DRIVER** boss will appreciate someone who does not bug them with trivialities which they should have been capable of solving themselves. Many times when I have found it necessary to send the memo due to needing funding or backing for my actions, the person I have sent the memo to has chosen to just circle and initial what he or she preferred me to do and sent me back the same sheet I sent him with the written comment "Do it!"

## Why Teaming Can Be Difficult

The majority of Americans have been educated in an atmosphere in which being a "Lone Ranger" is the normal way of life. Most aspects of our educational process are geared to a student working alone to accomplish his or her work. The teacher gives an assignment to the class and each student goes home, reads the textbooks alone, writes their essays alone, calculates their math problems alone and comes into class the next day ready to take a test alone. This process continues throughout the school experience and each student's grade depends on his or her individual study and involvement with the material of each class.

Once we complete our educational experience, we get a job in a company which is usually subdivided into different departments. Whether there are two or two hundred people in each department, every employee learns that individuals do not run a company alone. Marketing people need the assistance of accounting people. Salespeople need to work with those in shipping and receiving to assure products are delivered on time. Information Systems people need the input of those in all other departments and have a great deal of information to offer in return. We learn in the "real world," if we do not work together AS A TEAM similar to the crew in Star Trek, the job does not get done. Something can be missed and, overall, the family/company/community will suffer.

Employees, who worked as "Lone Rangers" for most of their school life, eventually learn people are different than they are. The work ethic for some people may not be as high as it is for others. Yet, without understanding what that difference is between people, we never get a chance to learn how to properly work with those people who are not like ourselves. Unfortunately, people from various faiths have to first get over that they are dealing with another human being; and that the color of a person's skin, their sexual orientation or culture does not dominate their abilities. We can learn from each person.

One of the key aspects of the "team" approach is that a certain synergy is created when more than one person works on a project. Specifically, this synergy, created by the team, is one which employs consensus to reach agreement. It is not good enough for the team to merely break the work up and complete the task. The approach assumes a team of three or four people working on a task can complete the task and then present a finished product of a quality which could not have been achieved by any one member of the team working alone. If in the past the projects required students to complete by individual effort and not team effort, many people may not be comfortable with the team experience. They might comment they would prefer to work on the project or task on their own. On a large project, this is not acceptable and is not cost or time effective for anyone including a company. Quite possibly, those people might have Analytical personalities and might be better used as research-ers for the rest of the team.

Team interaction has become essential in the workplace and any community project. Key advantages of the team process include: employees gaining knowledge and experience from each other in their work environments; individual strengths and weaknesses are blended as a sharing of teaching and learning responsibilities is facilitated; self-confidence and self-esteem are increased as leader-ship and participatory skills are developed; interpersonal commu-nication skills are strengthened and achievement of a higher level of quality and performance in project assignments is possible. The key elements of productive team members includes: Follow-through on commitments, open and honest communication among mem-bers, use of active listening skills and constructive resolution of conflicts and disagreements.

Once we learn how to work in a team we can accomplish great things. The well-known phrase everyone has heard is, "There is no 'I' in team." An army of soldiers can only be effective if they work as a team. Each soldier operating on his own may get someone killed. A group of medical doctors operating on someone's heart does so as a team, otherwise the patient may die. Any football fan knows there is no chance for their team to win if they do not work together towards one goal. Not everyone can be the one to either throw the ball or catch the ball and run for a touchdown.

There is an old story about a Christian minister of a medium size church who had problems with his board of directors and the other leaders of the church. Fighting was tearing the church apart and in prayer the minister got the message he needed to quickly turn things around. On Sunday he announced from the pulpit, "God came to me during the night and told me one of my congregants was the Messiah." He stated, "I was not told which congregant it was but it would be revealed to me soon." He asked his congregation, "Did God visit any of you and reveal who in our congregation is the Messiah?" No one knew and yet from that day on, every congregant treated each other with kindness, respect and love.

Imagine if you found out the person who is the greatest irritant to your soul, was the Messiah. How would you treat him or her from that moment on? Imagine how well a company would be run if everyone took personal responsibility to make sure each portion they were responsible for was done correctly. There would never be another Enron-type scandal. The Enron scandal was a series of events that resulted in the bankruptcy of the U.S. energy, commodities, and services company Enron Corporation and the dissolution of Arthur Andersen LLP, which had been one of the largest auditing and accounting companies in the world. It takes a shift in consciousness to go from a Lone Ranger to a team player. It takes a further shift to consider each one you meet to be holy. Once done, there is Peace in your life.

## Meditation

I actually have never liked the word meditation although I use it often. I prefer to call the act Planned Daydreaming. For many people, the word meditation connotes strange and nonproductive behavior. Due to the myths about meditation, many adults will not allow themselves to look deeper into the subject. However, I do not know another word which can more completely describe a planned daydream state of mind. In the faith world, meditation is also referred to as: Contemplative Prayer, Quiet Time, Introspection, Self-Reflection, Deep Thought/Concentration and other terms. It is all the same and almost every faith uses it.

People enjoy that portion of a fishing trip when they are alone and can allow their minds to relax and think of nothing. Busy men and women look for a place to "crash" so they can rid themselves of the day's stresses. Almost anyone you speak with, in or out of a TALK ZONE, will admit they would like to find a way to stop and clear their minds of their daily responsibilities even if just for a little while. If we can just get rid of some of the fallacies the word has come to represent, no matter what you call it, meditation is a valid answer.

The fallacies are many. I find that, to reach a deeper and higher level of consciousness, we DO NOT have to sit in the lotus position. We do not have to wear certain types of cotton clothing nor sit facing a specific direction. We do not have to burn incense or candles, and we do not have to be a vegetarian. Drinking herbal teas or avoiding sexual activity have nothing to do with meditation. There is no one way to meditate; and we do not have to belong to special churches or meditation groups to get the proper spiritual response.

Daydreaming, becoming one with ourselves, looking within, finding inner peace, praying, calling on a Higher Power for guidance, tapping into Universal Intelligence, meditating, or whatever we want to call a planned session of personal quiet can be the most important thing we can ever do for ourselves. This is our self-programming time when we develop personal goals and learn to expand our abilities. This is the time when we solve problems and work out physical and/or mental difficulties. In the meditative state we can go beyond space and time and all physical barriers. This is a time to love our self and ready our Oneness with ALL.

Isn't it time we gave more love to our self?

In order to get maximum results when we first begin to meditate, there are only two stipulations we need to adhere to — do not meditate when tired, and do not meditate in a room full of distractions. Eventually we will be able to meditate at any time and in any place.

The reason not to meditate when we are tired is, simply, we will fall asleep. If we are relaxing our body and mind so we can program ourselves for goal setting, the last thing we want to do is to fall asleep. Finding a time early in the morning, at lunch, or before or after dinner gives us a chance to get to know ourselves better and to program our self for a good rest when we do want to fall asleep.

If you choose to meditate at home and there are other people in the house, tell them you need their help. Ask them to respect your needs for privacy and quiet for the short time you will be meditating. If total quiet does not occur, do not stress yourself. Relaxation comes from internal quiet first.

What is internal quiet? Have you ever tried to fall asleep, but your mind kept wandering from one subject to the next? How am I going to pay that car insurance bill? How will I tell my boss I want a raise? What shall I tell my parents about the new "special" friend in my life who is not of our faith? This is NOT internal quiet. Internal quiet happens when you allow your mind to concentrate on only that which you want it to. Sometimes it can be difficult but it CAN be done.

If you find yourself having difficulty reaching internal quiet, try the following. Before you close your eyes, write down any major projects you are working on. They could be projects from work or home or from wherever. Be conscious of the fact you cannot achieve internal quiet when you have major projects on your mind. By writing them down you give them importance and you can be assured you will not forget those items. The list will be waiting for you when you finish your meditation. By doing this, you are mentally prioritizing your immediate life's projects and making way for internal quiet. You can also use the same process if you are having trouble falling asleep.

After you've found a comfortable place to sit or lie down, position yourself so one leg is not on top of another. This may cause a circulation problem you will have to attend to during your meditation. And now … RELAX!

REEEEELAXXX

Close your eyes and tell yourself to RELAX.

By telling yourself to relax, your mind listens to your mental command and has no choice but to relax. Take a deep, cleansing breath; fill your lungs to capacity. Breathe in through your nose and out through your mouth and know the air you are taking into your lungs is cleansing your body. Know your lungs and vital organs are receiving clean air which is necessary for their proper operation. Know each time you relax, your body regenerates itself and becomes healthier. Medical professionals endorse this type of breathing.

Mentally encircle your body with a white light of protection from God/Spirit/ your higher power, and know that that Power is helping you to relax and is protecting you in all you do.

Take a second deep breath and this time tell yourself "more and more relaxed." Allow your body to feel the relaxation coming into it. Inhale slowly and exhale at the same rate. This regulates your body's respiratory system and calms you even more. Now you are ready to begin the simplest relaxation program you will ever experience. There are no mysteries, no special incantations, no magic words, just the desire to become relaxed.

First, tell your feet to relax. Do not TRY to make them relax, just KNOW they are relaxing. (I remember my first try at meditation. I was paying too much attention to my body responding to the commands of "relax." My mind became preoccupied with the process and I found I could not relax.) Feel the relaxation spread slowly upward from the soles of your feet through your ankles, into your calves, your knees, up into your thighs, into your buttocks, and then up to your waist. Know every muscle, tendon, and fiber of your body from your waist down is completely relaxed. Feel each portion of your body relaxing and allow the relaxation to massage any tired or sore muscles into relaxed and healthy muscles. YOU are in control of your body relaxing. As the relaxation begins to spread upward from your waist, take another deep cleansing breath and feel your abdomen and all your inner organs relaxing. Feel your heart relax as you slowly release the air from your lungs and know your heart will work better because of this relaxation.

Allow the relaxation to move upward into your chest and shoulders and then down into each arm, into the biceps, the elbows, the forearms, the wrists, the hands, and into each finger of each hand. Know every muscle, tendon, and fiber of your body from the shoulders down is totally and completely relaxed.

Now allow the relaxation to spread upward from your shoulders into your neck, massaging your neck into total relaxation; into your jaw and face, relaxing all of your facial muscles; and then into your head so your entire body is completely and perfectly relaxed.

Feel a sense of total relaxation and remember it. Experience the pleasure of being in full relaxation and thank yourself for being there. When you first begin to meditate you may want to take five minutes or more getting to a full body relaxation. As you begin to get into a daily routine of meditation, you will eventually be able to reach this relaxed state in seconds.

What I do once my body has reached a full level of relaxation is to count backward from twenty to ten and to know my body is moving into a deeper and deeper level of relaxation with each descending number. I count down twenty ... nineteen ... eighteen ... deeper and deeper, seventeen ... sixteen ... fifteen ... more and more relaxed, fourteen ... thirteen ... twelve ... eleven and ten. At ten my body reaches what is called the Alpha Level of relaxation. If your body was hooked up to sensitive recording devices in a laboratory, scientists would say your brain is producing Alpha Rhythms. Now your mind has a chance to dream and program itself to do anything it needs or wants to do. This is the point where you can concentrate on your goals or solve problems which are bothering you. It may give you a solution to a problem you were not aware of.

You can spend as much time as you like in this stage of relaxation and, when you are ready to awaken, you can begin to program your actions for when you will return to the conscious level. Affirm for yourself, "I am handling all of my daily problems calmly" or "My Divine Power is handling all my problems." You can tell yourself your night's sleep will be very relaxed, and you will awaken the next morning refreshed and reenergized for the day. The options are limitless.

A slow count from ten to twenty brings you back to the conscious level very easily. Know always you are in full control of your relaxation and, if necessary, you can reach the conscious state in a second if you need. So let's count; ten ... eleven ... twelve ... feel your body getting stronger and stronger, thirteen ... fourteen ... fifteen ... feel your body getting healthier and healthier, sixteen ... seventeen ... eighteen ... your eyes are now beginning to open, nineteen ... twenty. You are now totally awake at the conscious level.

As we begin to expand our PEOPLEism abilities and communicate with others in TALK ZONES, it is important to be proficient in some type of meditation so you can have peaceful control of your mental and emotional processes most of the time. Having control can mean the difference between a happy life and an exceptionally fulfilling one. The more times you meditate, become peaceful, and transfer control to your waking hours, the easier it is to explore and expand your other abilities.

MEDITATION = CONTROL = HAPPINESS

# ABOUT THE AUTHOR

Rev. Dr. Stephen Albert is the Director of the World Interfaith Network (https://world-interfaith.com) and the co-minister with his wife Rev. Dr. Abigail of the All Faith Center (https://all-faithcenter.org) in Poway California. He is a founding member of the Poway Interfaith Team and was its President various years. For 44 years, Dr. Steve taught college classes in: Futurism, Critical Thinking, Communications, Public Speaking, Comparative Religion and many other subjects. He was an Architectural Designer for 25 years before he entered the ministry and he designed over 500 retail stores around the world. Rev. Steve is the author of 17 books including The Interfaith Manual, The Interfaith Workbook and the REBOOT Series of 8 books. He holds 3 college degrees and a Doctoral in Religious Studies from Emerson Theological Institute. He created and coordinated the New Thought conference booth at the 2009, 2015, & 2018 Parliament of World Religions. Dr. Steve was a facilitator at the Awakened World 2012 Dialogues in Rome and Florence, Italy. Steve serves on the Advisory Board of the Association of Global New Thought and Palomar College. He also created the yearly 'New Thought Day' holiday for the New Thought Faith. Rev. Steve chaired the North American Interfaith Network's Connect conference in San Diego in August of 2017 and for it, created Interfaith Awareness Week as a week-long celebration the second week in August each year. That San Diego County holiday became a California state celebration in 2018 and an American celebration in 2020. It is now celebrated in over 100 countries around the world. Steve has survived a major stroke, a 5-way bypass open heart surgery, and other physical issues which he was able to rehab from. Since 2004, Steve has volunteered his time once a week at Palomar Hospital's Acute Rehab Unit in Escondido, California, counseling stroke and other rehab patients and their families about getting well.

www.ingramcontent.com/pod-product-compliance
Lightning Source LLC
Chambersburg PA
CBHW070614060426
42445CB00038B/1176